The Bible and Reason

THE

AND
REASON

Anglicans and Scripture in Late
Seventeenth-Century England

GERARD REEDY, S.J.

UNIVERSITY OF PENNSYLVANIA PRESS
Philadelphia

Library of Congress Cataloging in Publication Data

Reedy, Gerard.
  The Bible and reason.

  Bibliography: p.
  Includes index.
  1. Bible—Criticism, interpretation, etc.—England—
History—17th century. I. Title.
BS500.R42 1985   220.6'0942   84-25608
ISBN 0-8122-7975-1

Printed in the United States of America

In memoriam
William J. Moody
eiusdem Societatis

Contents

Preface

ON THE 25th of May, 1660, a day whose memory echoes throughout the poetry and sermons of the succeeding age, Charles II landed at Dover, hoping to secure and hold the throne lost by his father. Old-time loyalists and newer office seekers accompanied him; among the latter was Samuel Pepys, the diarist, who recorded the first words of the king on landing. "The Mayor of the town came," Pepys wrote, "and gave him his white staffe, the badge of his place, which the King did give him again. The Mayor also presented him from the town a very rich Bible, which he took and said it was the thing he loved above all things in the world." [1]

One may be tempted to call the response of the king, who is not remembered principally for his biblical morality, a piece of playacting. In the next twenty-five years, preachers would often remind the king and his court of biblical morality, and wits would celebrate his lack of it. But the symbolism of the king's reception of the Dover Bible is not exhausted by noting his observance or nonobservance of the moral code it contained. Charles was not only accepting the Bible for himself but indicating a principle of his reign. He wanted to make clear that in his time the Bible would continue to be the rule and religion of English Protestants; in this gesture at Dover, England was accepting the English Bible for the English people. In 1638, in a work that became extremely influential after 1660, William Chillingworth wrote: "Nothing can challenge our beliefe, but what hath descended to us from Christ by Originall and Universall Tradition: Now nothing but Scripture hath thus descended to us, therefore nothing but Scripture can challenge our beliefe." [2] At Dover, accepting what he loved above all else in the world, the king reenacted the myth of the *sola Scriptura*, Scripture alone, the guiding life of the English church.

The Bible was the sole possession of no single theological party in late seventeenth-century England. Inside and outside the established church, theologians explored and argued how the Bible was to be interpreted; yet everywhere it was looked upon as the source not only of faith and morals but also of history and polity. The primacy of Scripture was a fact for both Puritans and Anglican churchmen, parliamentarians and royalists. Many of the Anglican churchmen, or "divines," whom Charles promoted in the church made a defense of the truth and integrity of Scripture their primary concern. Especially in the circles of the establishment, the late seventeenth century in England was an age obsessed with the formation of correct principles for interpreting the Bible. Too few historians who have written about this era have considered the study and defense of Scripture a particularly interesting index to the period.

One purpose of this book is to restore balance in our understanding of late seventeenth-century English thought through a discussion of some of the major preoccupations of scriptural interpreters who were members of the Church of England after 1660. In Appendix II, I have compiled a list of works that illustrate the bulk of writing between 1660 and 1700 on scriptural questions. The following chapters will, I hope, demonstrate the precision and richness of the thought of major and minor Anglican divines and laymen, particularly in regard to the principles by which the Bible may be known as true and may be correctly interpreted. Although able studies of theology after 1660 exist, there is no sustained discussion of the field of scriptural interpretation that I have chosen to explicate.[3]

My method is essentially one of exposition and ordering of primary texts concerning the various aspects of scriptural interpretation with which divines of the period were concerned. I am wary of any facilely constructed alliance between the "rationalism" of the Enlightenment and that of the divines whose writings make up the bulk of my primary texts. In his *History of English Thought in the Eighteenth Century*, a work still widely read, Leslie Stephen describes the late seventeenth-century Anglican divine as being "rationalist to the core."[4] The primary data cannot support such categorization. Likewise, Mark Pattison writes of these divines: "Reason was at first offered as the basis for faith, but gradually became its substitute. The mind never advanced as far as the stage of belief, for it was increasingly engaged in reasoning up to it."[5] My Chapters 2 and 3 demonstrate the conservatism of the divines in assigning meanings to "reason" as a means of understanding scriptural revelation. The divines were anything but "rationalist to the core," and their writings evidence a firm commitment to a "stage of belief" that both guided the reasoning faculty and isolated and defended areas of theology that reason could not comprehend. In the last century and even today, an urge exists to enlist as much seventeenth-century historical data as possible under a general progress toward "enlightenment."[6] The divines of late seventeenth-century England presented, in their complex use of reason to understand revelation, a historical problem that cannot be solved by a Whiggish interpretation of history.[7]

Although I disagree with the bias of Stephen and Pattison in treating the divines as a prelude to the Enlightenment, I join them in considering late seventeenth-century Anglican theology as an ordered body of thought. This book is not a study of individual authors but one of issues in scriptural interpretation addressed by several authors. My purpose is to show that late seventeenth-century Anglicanism was a coherent theological force, at least on the issues discussed here, built on what went before and alive to alternate movements of thought coexisting at the time.

Except in Chapter 4, I have generally avoided discussing the individual politics of the Anglican divines of the period. These authors' politics coincided with their religion at least to the extent that they remained in the established church after the Act of Uniformity of 1662. Nor have I discussed subsidiary political allegiances to the different governments under Charles II, to Latitudinarian or high church parties, or to William III after 1688 for such allegiances do not greatly impinge on the divines' common agreement on major questions of scriptural interpretation.

I have accepted the longstanding categorization of the Church of England as a *via media* between the theological right and left. In matters of scriptural interpretation, the right is the authority of Roman infallibility; the left is the Spirit-centered interpretation of disestablished and nonestablished churches and sects. Against both Rome and the sects, Anglicans formulated a rational interpretation of Scripture, which they hoped reasonable believers could accept and employ in the public forum. Even such a broad program involved political options: for example, the support of established universities to train rational theologians and of a sufficiently stable central government to leave them at peace to write their sometimes lengthy works. Within this middle-of-the-road political existence, various political and theological responses were possible, but differences tended to be muted when, against Roman Catholicism and the sects, divines argued their theories of scriptural truth and the interpretations that might build up that truth.

In the late seventeenth century, Anglican scriptural interpretation both strengthened and was strengthened by the political establishment. Rational interpretation of Scripture implies an arena of public argument and verification of its conclusions that is different from the private verification given by the Spirit. The divines insisted on the primacy of Scripture as the basis for theological truth; their stress on reason countered other methods of interpretation that they saw not only as unmanageably private but also as subversive of the establishment of church and state. The political establishment accordingly rewarded the theologians of the *via media*. Successful Anglican apologists were often made canons, deans, bishops, and archbishops. A theology written by university men, preached from distinguished pulpits in London and Oxford, and based on the Scripture read in the prescribed service was, not surprisingly, seen as an ally by the political arm. A theological project so dependent on an ordered society would not undermine it.

Besides the general context of the *via media*, I have also relied on a second context in which to understand the Anglican theology at issue: the secular interpretation of the Bible of Thomas Hobbes, Spinoza, and others. I have sought in part to perform an anatomy of rationalisms, to situate the thought of the divines on the Bible against that of secular philosophy. All Christian theology is, of its nature, a rational enterprise: it seeks to find or impose rational categories in or on the primary data of the Bible. To distinguish one variety of late seventeenth-century theology from another, one must pass beyond a simple distinction between "reason" and "revelation" and enter into an analysis of what "reason" means in the various ways it is used in exposition of scriptural doctrine. Was "reason" for the divines different from "reason" in the philosophical writings they felt compelled to answer? And, if so, how was it different? If such an anatomy of rationalisms could be performed on a body of literature consisting of doctrines alone, the task would be easy. For reasons that will become clear, doctrinal sameness and difference are not always adequate indexes to thought on Scripture during this period. Of equal importance is difference on the level of stated or assumed methodology, with which much of this book is concerned.

Parts of this book may be of interest only to specialist readers; questions of inspiration and canon, for example, are explored more because of the divines' interest in them than because such interest may revise our thought about the age. Other aspects of my discussion will be of more general interest. The ideas of Hobbes and Spinoza on Scripture, for example, have not been widely exposed, nor have the divines' responses. Students of John Locke will be interested in the similarity of his scriptural interpretation to that of the divines, which is explored in Chapters 4 and 6. Most important, I hope that the richness and comprehension of late seventeenth-century Anglican theology will become a permanent source of attraction for future historians, whatever their point of entry into the period.

The freedom to spend a year in research and writing this book was made possible by a fellowship granted by the American Council of Learned Societies and funded by the National Endowment for the Humanities and by a faculty fellowship from Fordham University. I am grateful for this essential support, and to those who helped me gain it, especially Sheridan Baker, Henry Knight Miller, and Ricardo Quintana.

I am indebted to the directors and staff of the following libraries: the Bodleian Library and Christ Church Library, Oxford; St. John's College Library, Cambridge; the British Library; Trinity College Library and Marsh's Library, Dublin; the Library of the Union Theological Seminary, New York, and Seth Kasten for his help in guiding me through the McAlpin Collection; the New York Public Library; and the Fordham University Library, where the availability and kindness of the staff know no bounds.

I am grateful to the following friends and scholars who have read all or part of the manuscript, correcting errors and suggesting changes: Francis Canavan, S.J., Donald J. Greene, Phillip Harth, Judith F. Hodgson, Margaret C. Jacob, Philip Judge, S.J., Paul J. Korshin, and Mary Ann Radzinowicz. The comments and corrections of these readers have, I hope, made this study better than it could have been had I been left to my own wits.

Anna Dal Pino, Cecelia Gazzola, and Victoria J. Maier typed parts of the manuscript. I am grateful to them and to Donald L. Magnetti, S.J., and Kevin B. McDonnell, whose generous hospitality in New York and London greatly lightened and enlivened a year of research and writing.

Over the past ten years, at regional and national meetings of the American Society for Eighteenth-Century Studies, I have had the opportunity to test and discuss many of the ideas governing this book; few members of the society can be as grateful as I am for its thriving existence. Finally, I owe a special debt of thanks for the guidance and encouragement given to me by Paul J. Korshin, Professor of English at the University of Pennsylvania, former Executive Secretary of ASECS, graduate teacher, and friend.

Fordham University
June 1984

1

A Moment in the History of Scriptural Interpretation

In 1657, only a few years before the Restoration of Charles II, a group of English scholars published the last of six folio volumes of the *Biblia Sacra Polyglotta*, the London Polyglot Bible. The publication partakes of the old and the new, forming a bridge from the Renaissance to the future uses English people would make of the Bible. Brian Walton, the general editor, had been a Laudian, as had others of his editorial collaborators; the London Polyglot stands as a monument to Archbishop William Laud's encouragement of Oriental learning, which outlasted his own trial and execution in 1644 and 1645. Printed in Latin, Greek, Hebrew, Arabic, Syriac, Hebraeo-Samaritan, Chaldean, Ethiopian, and Persian, with two hundred pages of prefatory material, the London Polyglot looked back to the Continental Renaissance tradition of enormous polyglots of great erudition and indeed borrowed liberally from their accumulated wisdom. The prefaces—on weights and measures, chronology, the geography of the Holy Land, the architecture of the Temple, and much more—summarized the careful research and guesswork of a hundred years of commentary.

Yet Walton and his collaborators knew that their project was different from any earlier effort. They believed that the copies of the ancient texts that they were printing were more authentic than those used in such previous polyglots as those of Antwerp (1569–72) and Paris (1628–45) and that the editing surpassed former efforts. "Effective awareness of the significance of textual criticism for the ancient versions of the biblical text," writes Basil Hall in *The Cambridge History of the Bible*, "may be said to begin only with the *Biblia Polyglotta* of Bishop Walton in 1657."[1] The London Polyglot was also easier to use. Walton had astutely arranged the different language versions of each book in parallel columns; in previous polyglots, the reader had to move from volume to volume to compare different versions of the same chapter or verse. Most important, Walton wanted to make his polyglot available. He announced in his 1652 prospectus that the future polyglot was to be different from all Continental versions, which could be afforded only by a prince.[2] If not a work for the common man, his Bible could be possessed, as a sign of devotion or affluence, by the upper classes. The London Polyglot not only was intended to show the world that the English were second to none in their scholarship; it self-consciously gave that scholarship wide circulation.

Indeed, references to Bishop Walton's work over the next forty years indicate that the strong, noble volumes lent an aura of psychological assurance to future scholars of Scripture. However adequately or inadequately the subscribers to the London Polyglot understood its achievement, the work let them feel that what they received as the Bible, what they heard read at service, and what they memorized at home was in fact based on the most authentic copies possible of the original writings dictated to Moses, David, or Paul by the Holy Spirit. This version was as near to the actual words of God as the noninspired reader could get. Because of the planning, advertising, and soliciting of subscriptions from 1652 on, the *Biblia Sacra Polyglotta* of 1657 was both a scholarly and a commercial success.

Walton was consecrated bishop of Chester in 1660 but died in 1661. Some of his collaborators on the London Polyglot continued to write, carrying on the tradition of linguistic and historical scholarship. John Lightfoot, a Presbyterian, had been Walton's editor for the Samaritan text of the Pentateuch; he conformed to the Church of England in 1662 and published, until his death in 1675, learned studies of the Gospels and Pauline writings, interpreting them in the light of rabbinical commentaries. Edward Pococke, a Laudian who worked on the Arabic text of the

Polyglot, published verse-by-verse commentaries on the minor prophets from 1685 until his death in 1691. After 1660, divines who had been too young to work on the Polyglot followed the scholarly path of its editors. Thus Simon Patrick, slowly making his way up through the church hierarchy in the 1670s and 1680s, crowned his life with two achievements: from 1691 on, he held the bishopric of Ely, one of the most desirable in England, and from 1695 on, he wrote and published ten volumes of Old Testament commentary. "Dr. Walton," wrote H. J. Todd, "had been working under a government which allowed him indeed *his paper free from duty*, but had deprived him of all his preferments."[3] By the end of the century, scholarly achievement in textual study had become the natural companion of ecclesiastical power and wealth.

Linguistic and historical commentary forms only one part of the richness of scriptural interpretation in late seventeenth-century England. Writings about Scripture were produced after 1660 in a great variety of modes and for a variety of audiences. Besides the work of scholars, simpler, more devotional works appeared, such as Robert Boyle's *Some Considerations Touching the Style of the Holy Scriptures* (1661); an experimentalist and natural philosopher, Boyle was also interested in making Scripture available to all, on a more popular level than Walton, and in this work taught the unsophisticated to cope with, among other problems, obscure passages of Scripture. Between 1660 and 1700, Anglicans also elaborated their traditional theory of the canon of Scripture, especially in response to the Roman Catholic thesis that only a central, infallible authority could designate canonical books. In this period also there was great interest in what the Bible says about forms of polity. This interest is evident in the writings of such major literary figures as Samuel Butler and John Dryden, along with many minor authors; their works frequently interpreted the religious and political changes of the age in biblical imagery. On a more philosophical level, debate about forms of secular polity often became arguments about interpreting the Old Testament. Thus John Locke's *Essay Concerning False Principles*, the first of his *Two Treatises of Government* (1690), is an extended rebuttal of Sir Robert Filmer's theory of kingship as a patriarchy; it is also, in essence, a treatise about how to relate Scripture, especially Genesis, to modern polity.

Scholarly commentary and political treatises alone, however, do not present the true character, the self-definition of Anglican scriptural interpretation in later seventeenth-century England. In a chronological bibliography of Anglican theological works written between 1660 and 1700, such as the catalog of the McAlpin Collection of the Union Theological Seminary in New York, or that of Dr. Williams's Library in London, the recurrence of the same key phrases and statements of project is striking. Such terms as "a rational account of the Scriptures" and "the reasonableness of belief in the Scriptures" appear again and again. Whatever these writers actually did to and for Scripture—and to define these accomplishments is a large part of the present work—they insisted that their project was "rational." They were trying to connect Scripture and reason in a new way or at least in a traditional way that they thought needed repeating in their age.

It is easy to misunderstand the Anglican theologians' insistence on the rationality of their project. It is particularly easy to excerpt passages from one or other of the divines to show how rationalistic they were, when fuller readings of the texts suggest subtler interpretations. The process of misleading quotation began early. On the title page of John Toland's *Christianity Not Mysterious* (1696), John Tillotson, the late archbishop of Canterbury, is quoted, in apparent justification of the author's radical theology; yet closer study of Tillotson's thought, and even of the context of the excerpted quotation, shows him in fundamental disagreement with the point of Toland's work.[4] Such excerpting and some of the categorizing to which it leads ignore many nuances and even major themes of the divines who wrote after 1660. Among the losses is the constant theme of Tillotson and others that, for all their own insistence on the reasonableness of scriptural Christianity, key scriptural doctrines like the Trinity and Incarnation were never intended to be understood as clear and distinct ideas; the hard core of revelation, that which revelation specifically reveals, is always above, though not contrary to, reason.

Much of late seventeenth-century Anglican theology footnotes the insights of William Chillingworth, who, in his *Religion of Protestants* (1638), maintained that, in possession of the gift of reason, we need neither Rome's authority nor the private inspirations of the sects to discover what

Scripture clearly teaches.[5] What this interpretative faculty is and what in Scripture is reasonable were questions that greatly exercised the generation after Chillingworth. It is always easier to define an extreme; the definition of a middle way often must work by trial and error, waiting until one's position is challenged, and by subsequent redefinition. Anglican theologians after 1660 sustainedly discussed "reason" because, following Chillingworth, they considered a "rational account" the obvious, commonsensical course in sectarian controversies. In this sense, "reason" as used by the divines had little to do with the growing rationalism of later seventeenth-century England and Europe.

The divines, however, were not ignorant of this wider context. As a moment in the history of scriptural interpretation, the later seventeenth century is of epochal interest. The ideas of a number of lay philosophers concerning Scripture—among them Lord Herbert of Cherbury, Thomas Hobbes, Spinoza, and John Toland—became current in England. These philosophers began to examine the truth of Scripture in a new way, without the inherited need to justify in it a preconceived list of *credenda*. In the next chapter I will outline their new secular methodologies. One important innovation they made was to attempt to divorce reason and Scripture. In 1670, Spinoza confidently asserted: "We must draw the absolute conclusion that the Bible must not be accommodated to reason, nor reason to the Bible."[6] Scripture is thought, in this scheme, not to teach the truth—which occurs only in philosophical statements—but merely to inculcate obedience. Spinoza's statement, unique in this period only for its candor, spelled the end of the sure accommodation of reason and scriptural revelation that had been the central theological tradition of Europe.

When late seventeenth-century Anglicans praised the reasonableness of Scripture, they were not trying to keep step with an increasingly rationalist cultural milieu. Their praises were not another attempt, doomed by historical change, to write a "liberal" theology. The divines rightly perceived that a long tradition of rational theology, available to them at least in the writings of Thomas Aquinas and, in England, of Richard Hooker, was entering a critical phase. To counter an abrupt dismissal of previous belief, the divines were forced to insist, sometimes stridently, on the rationality of revelation. Yet one misinterprets the Anglican divines of the later seventeenth century if one does not understand that their insistence on the reasonableness of Christianity was an iron grip not on a deistic future but on the traditional past.

II

In the following chapters, I have generally relied on the writings of four major divines to represent Anglican scriptural interpretation in the later seventeenth century, although many other divines and laymen are quoted to establish the more nuanced details of the picture. These four divines are Isaac Barrow (1630–77), master of Trinity College, Cambridge; Robert South (1634–1716), prebendary of Westminster and canon of Christ Church, Oxford; Edward Stillingfleet (1635–99), bishop of Worcester and, I believe, the keenest Anglican theological mind of the last part of the century; and John Tillotson (1630–94), archbishop of Canterbury. These major divines form a "school" in a number of ways. There is evidence of personal association, especially among the three Cambridge men, Barrow, Stillingfleet, and Tillotson. After Barrow's early death, Tillotson loyally undertook the editing of his theological works, which appeared between 1683 and 1687. Tillotson's *Rule of Faith* (1666) is dedicated to Edward Stillingfleet, who provided a confirmatory afterword. When in the early 1690s clergy who had not sworn allegiance to William III attacked Tillotson for alleged Socinian leanings, Stillingfleet responded by giving a major anti-Socinian sermon from the pulpit at St. Lawrence Jewry that Tillotson had made famous[7] and by defending the archbishop's views, after his death in 1694, in further anti-Socinian writing.[8] An unknown editor aptly caught the mutuality of the anti-Socinian project in a pamphlet of 1697, *A Seasonable Vindication of the Blessed Trinity*, composed exclusively of excerpts from the writings of Stillingfleet and Tillotson but without separate identification.

The ecclesiastical world of the 1660s and after was not large. In addition to cooperative projects, discussions in various synods and convocations about the Prayer Book or church comprehension brought major and minor divines together. The existence of a "school" is also evident from the arguments used by many divines that are most thoroughly expressed in the writings of Barrow, South, Stillingfleet, and Tillotson. Robert South, the only Oxford man among these four divines, occasionally argued with the others.[9] Yet the content of South's own sermons shows him in fundamental agreement in matters of scriptural interpretation. South has a way of summing up, in a short space, the core of the communal apologetic. South may have been part of a "high church" and Stillingfleet and Tillotson of a "broad church" party. Such categorizations, however accurate, have no real meaning in the matter of scriptural interpretation. On the truth of Scripture, on reason and revelation, on miracles, on the uses of biblical typology in secular matters, on the question of canon, and on the critical doctrines of the Trinity and Incarnation, many other divines followed the clear and united pattern set by the four major enunciators of Anglican theology in the later seventeenth century.

III

Because each of the following chapters deals with a particular aspect of scriptural interpretation, some general characterizations regarding the broad scope of the rational scriptural theology of the Anglican divines of the later seventeenth century may be helpful.

If one assumes the traditional division, that the senses of Scripture are fourfold—literal, allegorical or typological, tropological, and anagogical—the divines were in the main concerned with the literal sense. In this they followed the Erasmian tradition that had held sway in the English and Continental renaissance of scriptural studies. From the English point of view, the London Polyglot of 1657 and the Authorized Version of 1611 provided the necessary materials for establishing the literal sense. Using both or at least the latter, the literate cleric or layperson could, without the help of commentaries, come into contact with the literal and saving truths of Scripture. These saving truths are, moreover, few and clear. They are not shrouded beneath textual or hermeneutical difficulties. Even though all of Scripture was held to be inspired, it was not doubted that many doctrines were ambiguous and might be the grounds for extensive debate as to their precise meaning. But God would not allow the believer's salvation to depend on such ambiguities; he had inspired the sacred writers to be eminently clear about the all-important truths. "Can any Man in his senses imagine," writes Stillingfleet, "that Christ's coming into the World to dye for Sinners, and the Precepts of a holy Life which he hath given, and the motives thereto from his second coming to judge the World, are not more plain than the Apocalyptic Visions, or the proofs for the Church of *Romes* Infallibility?"[10]

Nor did Anglicans think the mistaking of inessentials for essentials to be only a Roman Catholic problem. Samuel Butler submitted that Presbyterian Hudibras also misplaced his exegetical energies:

What Adam dreamt of when his Bride
Came from the Closet in his side:
Whether the Devil tempted her
By a *high Dutch* Interpreter:
If either of them had a Navel;
Who first made Musick malleable:
Whether the Serpent at the Fall
Had cloven Feet, or none at all.
All this, without Gloss or Comment,
He would unriddle in a Moment
In proper terms, such as men smatter
When they throw out and miss the matter.[11]

The presence in *Hudibras* of acts of scriptural interpretation that "miss the matter" of Scripture is significant. The First Part of *Hudibras*, where this passage occurs, was a popular poem; it achieved the distinction of appearing in four pirated editions within a year of its authorized publication. Satire becomes this popular only when the reader can readily identify the satiric voice and when that voice's discriminations of right from wrong accord with the public taste; in the early 1660s, the objects of Butler's satire, including Hudibras's misplaced efforts at scriptural interpretation, appear to have been widely shared objects of public disfavor.

A broad range of later seventeenth-century writers, including some in controversy with one another about other matters, shared this general assumption about the clarity of the doctrine that Scripture indubitably teaches. From Hooker and Chillingworth on, this assumption formed the basis for all Anglican discussion of Scripture. But it also figured strongly in the theories of scriptural truth of Herbert of Cherbury, Hobbes, Spinoza, and Toland. Herbert and Spinoza are especially prominent for their minimal lists of those truths clearly taught in Scripture. Moreover, historians have often noted a movement toward "plain style" in the sacred and secular fields throughout the later seventeenth century. In the sermons of the divines, this movement took the form of a reaction against the "metaphysical" style of such earlier preachers as John Donne and Launcelot Andrewes.[12] Although this movement is intelligible as a literary counterpart of the empiricism of the New Science, it also has a theological dimension. If God has assured that the revelation of essential matters in Scripture be plain and contained in its literal sense, then plain style begins to have a validity of its own, as the divinely chosen way of communicating in Scripture or otherwise.

Indeed, the divines went one step further. As the century progressed, the apologetics of the English Socinians, or Unitarians, gained force and clarity. Various meanings of the term "Socinian" are difficult to clarify, even as they were used in the later seventeenth century. In regard to the essential doctrines in Scripture, Socinians were united in maintaining that when Scripture seems to teach doctrines that, like the Trinity and the Incarnation, are not clear and distinct, the interpreter is forced to assume that metaphor is being employed. This exegetical tactic is discussed in the last chapter of this book. In responding to the Socinians, the divines refused to countenance this backsliding from the literal sense of the text. The subsequent controversy, which continued throughout the 1690s, revealed that the divines' commitment to the literal sense was deep, even when the price of maintaining that commitment was controversy which the doctrine of essential doctrines was partly forwarded to avoid.

The divines generally ignored the anagogical sense of Scripture, even though apocalyptic interpretation did not die with the waning of political power of the sects in the late 1650s.[13] In two contexts the typological sense of Scripture remained commonplace after 1660. The divines often discussed the typological meaning of Old Testament prophecies relative to the Messiah; this is typological interpretation in a strict sense. They were more wary of the secondary typology of king and state. Although they clearly knew about and occasionally adverted to the typology of England, like Israel an elected nation, typology was most appealing to the poets of the Stuart Restoration, and some minor divines, who used it without irony. The major divines, especially Robert South, were rigorously antienthusiast. They feared a recurrence of privatistic and sectarian scriptural interpretation: of the apocalyptic and typological readings that characterized, for the divines, the Interregnum, and that were thought to legitimize sedition. Of the last of the four senses of Scripture, the tropological or moral, much was made in the preaching of the divines, as in the preaching of any age. It is a mistake, however, to characterize late seventeenth-century scriptural interpretation as only moralistic. The following chapters tend to ignore tropological readings in favor of the rules for scriptural interpretation the divines elaborated from the literal sense.

The doctrine of the plain sense and the essentials therein contained did not excuse the divines from a defense of all of Scripture: doctrine, history, law, and prophecy. Their project was extremely ambitious. It attempted a rational undergirding not only of doctrines such as the immortality of the soul and the satisfaction paid by Christ; it claimed that rational accounts might also be given of the truth of such scriptural genres as the Mosaic history and prophetic visions. Within the context of the church service, the sermons of the divines generally dealt with the simpler matter of the explication of doctrine and morals. In their more academic tracts and books, the divines worked at the more demanding task of a rational discussion of all of Scripture. The integrity of the whole of Scripture, in all its parts, was both the assumption and the goal of such discussion, even when the categories of history and prophecy, unlike that of doctrine, did not obviously ally themselves with a rational defense. During the seventeeth century, rationalist scriptural interpretation had begun to abandon certain genres of the Bible as rationally indefensible; the divines maintained the more traditional position that all of Scripture can be rationally defended, if men have the wit.

Anglican scriptural interpretation at this time was deeply controversial. Mark Pattison's nineteenth-century caricature is only slightly exaggerated: "Every one who had anything to say on sacred subjects drilled it into an array of argument against a supposed objector. Christianity appeared made for nothing else but to be 'proved'; what use to make of it when it was proved was not much thought about."[14] The divines, of course, did not think their opponents to be "supposed." Roman Catholics, Presbyterians, deists, and Socinians were living opponents. Moreover, the theological views of these parties often had political overtones which Anglicans perceived as a threat to the delicate balance of Restoration polity. The divines were utterly *engagés*; their individual writings were keyed to the recent appearance of a pamphlet or book and may seem overly argumentative and querulous today.

The controversial nature of the divines' writings also relates to the need for a sense of context; it is sometimes essential to interpret individual statements in the light of the "supposed objector." If the divines seem excessive in their praise of rational religion, it may be that a Roman Catholic apologist was near, to cast doubt on the integrity of Scripture; or perhaps deism was at hand, ready to submit a minimal list of *credenda*, dismissing all else as irrational. If the "mystery" of Scripture is stressed, Socinian objectors—who denied the presence of mystery in Scripture— may have been in the wings. A sense of the precise controversy going on, a fairly careful notion of context, balances isolated and apparently extreme statements against one another.

The divines of the later seventeenth century, especially Edward Stillingfleet, occasionally proclaimed their independence of René Descartes. Yet their writing suggests a profound dependence on his work. The doctrine of essentials, which is pre-Cartesian, has a natural affinity with a theory of clear and distinct ideas. The preoccupation of the divines and their Roman Catholic adversaries with "certainty" speaks of a more directly Cartesian inheritance. Most of all one catches the flavor of Descartes in the many statements of the divines concerning the inviolability of the natural ideas that God has given to the human mind. "God never perswades a Man of any thing," writes Tillotson, "that contradicts the Natural and Essential Notions of his Mind and Understanding. For this would be to destroy his own Workmanship, and to impose that upon the Understanding of a Man, which whilst it retains its own nature, and remains what it is, it cannot possibly admit." [15] In the area of scriptural interpretation, this commitment to the affinity of revelation and the human mind worked in various directions. It led to the denial of certain scriptural doctrines, or at least an attempt to explain them away, when they appeared to violate innate ideas and norms of rationality. This was the way of Herbert of Cherbury and Toland; it was the cornerstone of Socinian interpretation of Scripture. The way of the divines led elsewhere: to a deeply held assumption that whatever is in Scripture, God's revelation, could not be conceived to confound God's coordinate gift, human reason.

A self-conscious Cartesian foundation does not seem to make a promising beginning for a theological project as vast as the divines contemplated for a full explication of scriptural faith and history. Mathematical certainty and methodical doubt hardly provide a suitable point of departure for a full and rational defense of scriptural faith. Descartes himself did not pretend to be a theologian in this wider sense. Of the mysteries of Scripture he has little to say, except that God may reveal matters, like the Trinity and Incarnation, which we may not clearly understand.[16] It is something else again to try to retain Cartesian categories and enter into an extended discussion of such mysteries. The difficulties in casting these—the preexistence of the Logos, the Incarnation, the Trinity, and the satisfaction paid by Christ—into clear and distinct ideas seem insuperable.

How did the Anglican divines of the later seventeenth century confront this problem? On the one hand, they tried, in various ways, to rationalize the mysteries of scriptural Christianity. They showed that such mysteries confirmed rather than denied the ideas of God's infinity and goodness innate in the human mind. Moving beyond Descartes, they showed how, if the manner of existence of such mysteries could not be rationally understood, the fact of their existence could be. They carefully distinguished between various types of certainty, attempting to fulfill the letter if not the spirit of Descartes. Their methodology strained its own categories especially when they repeatedly asserted the "moral" evidence for the certainty of biblical history and doctrine.[17] Such evidence at times does not appear to ground "certainty," and a number of contemporary writers clearly did not accept the argument.

On the other hand, did the divines attempt to have it both ways? Did they claim the Cartesian inheritance at the same time that they altered it out of recognition? They wanted rationally to undergird Scripture, a traditional project, but they wanted to do so in the best modern terms. Jan Walgrave, a recent historical theologian, calls the bluff of seventeenth-century "Latitudinarianism." "Once reason in whatever form is accepted as the only principle of theological hermeneutics," he writes, "the way lies open to the negation of Christianity, and theology itself is emptied."[18] Walgrave's point of view is perhaps too critical and too sure of itself, after the fact. More important, the meanings of "reason" are many; surely some of its forms present less of a challenge to Christianity. One must always remember that thousands of intelligent men and women lived and believed the Scripture as it was taught and preached to them by the divines of the later seventeenth century. Nevertheless, Walgrave has put his finger on a real problem in any attempt to understand late seventeenth-century Anglican theology. The divines, especially Edward Stillingfleet, addressed the irreconcilability of some kinds of reason and scriptural revelation. Yet because they used the words "reason" and "rational" so lavishly and so proudly, they seem, much of the time, to be ignoring some of the problems in methodology that their announced intentions bring up. Were the divines in fact coy? Did they merely play at Cartesianism and scriptural mystery, only to abandon one or the other at their convenience? Are the interpretational problems they present to Walgrave and others only latter-day criticisms, or does their project betray throughout irreconcilable allegiances? Only a full encounter with the scriptural theology of the divines permits us to begin to answer these questions.

2

The Argument from Internal Evidence: Herbert of Cherbury, Hobbes, Spinoza, Toland, and the Divines

Is Scripture true? If so, in what sense is it true? By what analogy do we compare the truth of Scripture to the truth of other objects of mind and sense? Is it as true as something we can see or feel? As true as the predictable sum of the angles of a triangle or the ratio of the circumference to the diameter of a circle? Is it true because we believe its authors or because something inherent in it compels assent? If Scripture is true in any of these ways, what about it is true? Its history, its doctrine, its prophecy, its miracles? Believers in the twentieth century tend to regard these questions as having been settled sometime in the past; we do not wish to go through the arguments again and, if we are at all interested, prefer to move immediately to more scriptural and less philosophical questions. In the seventeenth century, however, such questions were considered very important, indeed, the very purpose of rational theology. Until they were answered, it was thought, a theological project was a house built on sand. The theology of late seventeenth-century Anglican divines, our topic here, generally lacks richness in the areas of grace, of the sacraments, of sin, and of liturgy. Part of this poverty is explained because these divines poured so much of their energy elsewhere—into an extended apologetics about the truth of Scripture.

Such apologetics were stimulated, in this period, by secular philosophy, which posed challenging and unorthodox questions about how

Scripture was true. This seventeenth-century philosophical critique of Scripture did not set out to destroy its credibility. Like many progressive intellectual movements, it attempted to distill the best of traditional thought and to carry this to the refreshment of a new age. In this period, as in many others, liberal theology's last self-defense was a good one: only when believers isolate the rationally certain in Scripture can they truly encounter an atheism based on reason alone. Yet such rational defense of Scripture is perilous business. A fine line exists, at times, between rational scriptural theology and a rationalist undermining of scriptural authority. Four seventeenth-century authors crossed the line in regard to Scripture, in the eyes of many, into rationalism: Herbert of Cherbury, Hobbes, Spinoza, and John Toland. As a group, they outlined two ways in which reason had begun to supplant Scripture as the source of religious truth in the later seventeenth century.

In *De Religione Laici* (1645), Herbert of Cherbury tells us that he has found "the pure and undisputed word of God" in Scripture.[1] He means that he has found a rational content in Scripture so sure that no one can disagree with it. This content involves his five "Catholic truths" or "common notions" concerning religion: (1) there is a God, (2) to whom worship is due, (3) in acts of faith, love, and virtue, and (4) repentance for sin, which (5) will be rewarded or punished in an afterlife. Not only Scripture holds these truths. Before and during the rational person's discovery of them there, they may also be found first within himself, by the action of God on his mind, and second, in "universal wisdom," an abstraction which right reason has discovered to be verified in a number of religious systems. Most important, the five truths are not sectarian: they "by no means depend on some faith or tradition, but have been engraved on the mind by God, and . . . have been considered and acknowledged as true throughout the world, in every age."[2]

Since the five truths do not seem clearly Christian, the "faith and tradition" which Herbert professes in his works, one reasonably inquires about the more precise relationship of these truths to the Christian Scriptures. Herbert offers several ways of answering such an inquiry. He expects that other doctrines will be added to these notions by the "genuine dictates of faith,"[3] an expectation that surely allows room for more explicitly Christian doctrine. He also says that he holds fast to all that the

English church of his birth believes, but that all its theology leads to the five common notions: "I found," he writes, "that all Misteryes Sacraments and Revelations cheefely tended to the Establishment of these five Articles as being at least the principall end for which they were ordeyned."[4] One cannot tell whether, in writing of "five Articles," Herbert alludes to the many more "articles" his church required for belief. Though seventeenth-century theologians of many backgrounds favored simple statements of necessary doctrine, Herbert's reduction of thirty-nine articles to five suggests an intellectual operation which many in the Anglican "faith or tradition" might not wish to follow. The verb phrase "cheefely tended" is also ambiguous in that it may or may not be reductionist. Herbert did not choose here or elsewhere to explicate the exact differences between his natural religion and the Anglican scriptural faith of the Trinity and the Incarnation. In *De Veritate* (1624), an early work, he writes of his five truths that "the book, religion, and prophet which adheres most closely to them is the best"; great care must be exercised in departing from these "principles of common reason."[5]

Since Herbert presented his philosophy somewhat unsystematically in a series of essays over several years, one can only infer, from various passages, the possible relationship of his five notions to Scripture. From the point of view of a philosophical anthropology, these notions seem to be the essence of Christianity and of a number of other religions. They form the "principal ends" of Scripture for the philosophically minded who seek general ideas that exist in a number of creeds. But they seem to be more forceful. The notions may also be interpreted as a rational norm for reading Scripture; that which does not accord with them, in Scripture, would seem to have a lesser value as truth. If the five notions contain the principal truth of Scripture, and if all else in Scripture is of some lesser authority, then we may reasonably say that Herbert was reaching out for the proposition that was expressed more clearly later in the century: that reason, in the sense of a faculty that deals in general ideas, is a competent judge to decide what is or is not truth in Scripture. In other words, we cannot say, without distinguishing, that all parts of Scripture are equally true. After 1660 Anglican divines commonly said that God would not reveal in Scripture something contradictory to what he had revealed of himself, in ideas innate to the human mind—though Scripture may reveal things above and superior to those innate preparations for truth. Herbert does not draw the matter so finely; the five common notions suggest that reason in a somewhat narrow sense is the full judge of the truth of Scripture.[6]

Whereas Herbert reached out toward one type of the new seventeenth-century rationalism about scriptural truth, Hobbes reached out toward the other in *Leviathan* (1651). Hobbes suggests in several places that Scripture asks for, in its hearers or readers, not "rational knowledge" but simply "belief." Recent study of Hobbes's own religious belief has accentuated its positive content. As Paul J. Johnson has argued, the religion of *Leviathan* is intelligible as a variant of the advanced but orthodox religious thought of John Hales and William Chillingworth of the Great Tew circle, a circle of intellectual ferment meeting in the 1630s at the country house of Lucius Cary, Viscount Falkland, and of which Hobbes was a member. Hobbes's "treatment of religious matters is firmly grounded in his full acceptance of the simplified Christianity developed by moderate Anglicans like Hales and Chillingworth."[7] Such "simplified Christianity" was a major force, in the period, in dividing scriptural matter into "necessary" doctrine, which pertained to the believer's salvation, and doubtful or obscure matters, which might be left to specialists to decide. "Scripture is given to all to learn," writes Hales in 1617, "but to teach, and to interpret, only to a few."[8] The Great Tew theologians hesitated to list the matters Scripture taught as necessary to be believed for salvation. They were also careful not to say that these matters are true in some sense different from other matters in Scripture. Should their list of necessary matters be extant, however, it would certainly include more specifically Christian doctrines, like the Trinity and Incarnation, than appear in Herbert's attenuated list.

Whatever its orthodoxy in a specifically Anglican sense, *Leviathan* adumbrates the doctrine fully enunciated by Spinoza, twenty years later, concerning the essential distinction between "faith" and "knowledge":

The Scripture was written to shew unto men the kingdom of God, and to prepare their minds to become his obedient subjects; leaving the world, and the philosophy thereof, to the disputation of men, for the exercising of their natural reason. Whether the earth's, or sun's motion make the day, and night; or whether the exorbitant actions of men, proceed from passion, or from the devil, so we worship him not, it is all one, as to our obedience and subjection to God almighty; which is the thing for which the Scripture was written.[9]

Hobbes recognized that the Bible makes statements about astronomy and psychology, but there was no need to be concerned with the truth of these statements. The purpose of the Bible is to help us obey God. From other parts of *Leviathan*, it appears that Hobbes, somewhat inconsistently, did not question the truth of the scriptural narrative of Jewish history or even of its accounts of miracles; whether he considered such narratives factual, or simply stimuli to obedience, or both, is not clear. What is clear is Hobbes's attempt to ward off certain criticisms that could be made of the Bible from the point of view of natural philosophy. To do this he exempts parts of Scripture, in a somewhat different way from Herbert, from the category of scientific knowledge. An elaborate diagram Hobbes draws of "the several Subjects of Knowledge" in chapter 9 of *Leviathan* more broadly indicates his direction: in this scheme, neither theology, the Bible, nor revelation is given a place.

Even if the Bible or parts of it are not science, why do we accept its message of obedience as true? If internally rational verifications are wanting, what external factors give the Scriptures authority? When the divines of the later seventeenth century approached this problem, though they did not deny internal proof, they created an involved proof of the truth of Scripture from the authority of the writers. *Leviathan*'s answer to the problem is concrete and commonsensical:

It is manifest . . . that Christian men do not know, but only believe the Scripture to be the word of God; and that the means of making them believe, which God is pleased to afford men ordinarily, is according to the way of nature, that is to say, from their teachers. . . . the ordinary cause for believing that the Scriptures are the word of God, is the same with the cause of believing of all other articles of our faith, namely, the hearing of those that are by law allowed and appointed to teach us, as our parents in their houses, and our pastors in the churches.[10]

Hobbes domesticates, as it were, the rational problem, reducing the problem of proof which so exercised the divines to an instance of Christian nurture. Hobbes allows that the rational inquirer may try to establish the truth of Scripture for himself. Yet *Leviathan* gives no assurance that such inquiry will ever go beyond "belief" to "knowledge." In his discussion of belief, Hobbes leaves no doubt as to its object: not internal content but the credibility of the person enunciating the matter for belief.[11] He does not enter into the question, as did the divines, of whether this credibility itself may be the object of rational inquiry. His desire to explain the presence of Christian belief in terms of the state, an explanation in accord with the general thrust of *Leviathan*, accounts for this absence of discussion; *Leviathan* nevertheless indicates that belief always remains subjective, lacking constituent rational grounds.

In the *Tractatus Theologico-Politicus* (1670), the most rigorously philosophical critique of Scripture written in the later seventeenth century, Spinoza states as his purpose the full separation of philosophy from theology that was hinted at in Hobbes.[12] Reason tells us certain truths about God: one God exists, omnipresent and with supreme right and dominion; worship of him consists of justice, charity, and love of one's neighbor; these accomplished, we are saved, and God also forgives those who repent. These truths are both "the dogmas of universal faith" and "the fundamental dogmas of Scripture."[13] But reason alone determines them, and Scripture gives only moral support to their observance.

The great interest of the *Tractatus* lies elsewhere than in this summary of natural religion. Spinoza's main contribution to the history of scriptural interpretation in the period is twofold. First, he insisted that Scripture be read on its own terms: "The meaning of Scripture is only made plain through Scripture itself."[14] To understand an individual book, we must understand its "history": its author, its cultural matrix, its genre, and its language. We must not assume, for example, that the prophets and historians of Scripture agreed on the subjects of which they wrote; each book tells its own story. Using this methodology, Spinoza discovered or rediscovered that Moses could not have written the entire Pentateuch, that "the prophets were in certain respects ignorant," that the chronology of Old Testament history is corrupt, and so on.[15]

Second, because of the unreliability of the authors of its historical and prophetic books, Scripture in no way, by itself, offers us certain knowledge, either of scientific and historical matters or even of God. Knowledge of God occurs only in "general ideas"; the imaginative particularity of scriptural history and prophecy, except indirectly, cannot, of its nature, present us with such ideas. Miracles especially distressed Spinoza because their singularity affronts the general laws by which God governs the universe. What, then, is the purpose of Scripture? Spinoza repeats Hobbes's suggestion: Scripture "demands nothing from men but obedience and censures obstinacy, but not ignorance"; "the aim and the object of Scripture is only to teach obedience"; the "doctrine of the Gospels enjoins nothing but simple faith, namely, to believe in God and to honor Him, which is the same thing as to obey Him." Spinoza carries this line of thought very far: even if a scriptural doctrine is false, "though there be many such which contain not a shadow of truth," it is useful if it inculcates obedience. Spinoza consistently rejected one rationalist canon: that only what conforms to right reason in Scripture is true: "Philosophy has no end in view save truth; faith, as we have abundantly proved, looks for nothing but obedience and piety." Philosophy fails only in that it does not lend moral imperatives to its findings about how religious people should behave. Only the "special grace of God" in Scripture can add the dimension of obligation. Thus Spinoza considers "the utility and the need for Holy Scripture or Revelation to be very great."[16] But Scripture does not satisfy the need for knowledge or certainty, which only philosophy provides.

More than twenty years after publication of the *Tractatus*, John Toland commenced his own interpretations of Scripture with a work very much in the rationalist vein of Herbert of Cherbury. Borrowing many of its ideas from Locke's *Essay Concerning Human Understanding* and the Socinian tracts of the early 1690s, *Christianity Not Mysterious* (1696) is unambiguous in its statement of one rationalist hypothesis about Scripture: there is no mystery in Scripture and all of its contents are available to reason. "All the Doctrines and precepts of the New Testament (if it be indeed Divine) must consequently agree with *Natural Reason*, and our own ordinary Ideas." The inviolability of reason, a gift from God, must be strictly observed. The argument that proves the truth of Scripture from the authority of the speaker is to be repudiated: the divines "prove the Authority and Perfection before they teach the Contents of Scripture; whereas the first is in great measure known by the last." The proof for Scripture's truth is internal. Toland also reiterates Spinoza's doctrine about studying Scripture without prejudice: "Nor is there any different Rule to be fol-low'd in the Interpretation of *Scripture* from what is common to all other Books." The structure of *Christianity Not Mysterious* makes its blunt point: what reason is (Part I), that nothing in the Gospel is contrary to reason (Part II), or above it (Part III): "We hold that Reason is the only Foundation of all Certitude; and that nothing reveal'd, whether as to its *Manner* or *Existence*, is more exempted from its Disquisitions, than the ordinary Phenomena of Nature." [17]

When Toland so chose, as in his slightly later work on the canon of Scripture, he could amass historical evidence in support of an argument; *Christianity Not Mysterious* is the work of a cultivated intellect speaking through a brash and cocky persona. It ably popularized the rational prem-ise, without footnotes or calculated obscurities, that reason alone is to be the norm of revelation. It disregards distinctions between faith and knowl-edge drawn by others; there does not seem to be any distinction between them in Toland's scheme.

Because Toland so clearly and aprioristically made reason the norm of revelation and denied "mystery" a place in this scheme, his methodology is rationalist. Even if no very accurate knowledge is gained by drawing a line of the progress of "deism" from Herbert to Toland, both surely shared the same broad vision—a reductionist frame of reference in which the fewer and the more in accordance with reason the truths of Scripture are shown to be, the better. What I have called a second type of ration-alism in regard to Scripture is perhaps more difficult to understand pre-cisely as rationalism. Hobbes and Spinoza proposed not that revelation be rationalized but that revelation has little or nothing to do with reason. Such a proposition depends on the fundamental division in human cogni-tion that they made. Faith, based on the evidence of testimony, moves in one direction; reason, based on other evidence, moves elsewhere. The knowledge and interpretation of Scripture belong entirely in the first category. Is this division of knowing a rationalism? The categorization is perhaps not as clear in Hobbes as in Spinoza. For in the *Tractatus,* the knowledge—if it can be called that—gained through faith in Scripture is clearly inferior to that gained through the general ideas enunciated by reason alone. Even if Scripture is of great religious use, Spinoza devalues it to something affecting only the will, which is divorced, in this instance, from human reason, which has a necessary preeminence over every other faculty.

II

One clear and concise account of the Anglican efforts, in the later seventeenth century, to maintain a traditional entente between reason and faith occurs in Joseph Glanvill's *Essays on Several Important Subjects in Philosophy and Religion* (1676). In many of the areas he was interested in and wrote about, Glanvill tended to broaden and explain the insights and projects of others; that he was more popularizer than unique thinker makes his work an all the more valuable index to Anglican thought after 1660. In the 1676 *Essays*, Glanvill represents, in brief, the general Anglican effort not to let reason and revelation slip apart. The titles of essays 4 and 5, "The Usefulness of Philosophy to Theology" and "The Agreement of Reason to Religion," suggest Glanvill's opposition to the Spinozan divorce, fully enunciated in 1670, of reason and faith. Glanvill's advocacy of a reasonable Christianity is thus a conservative effort to restore the balance between reason and faith that had recently been challenged.

For Glanvill, philosophy is an ancillary science to theology; that is, the scriptural truths of Christianity are made more firm by the secondary support they receive from philosophical analysis. For example, in the fourth essay, he shows how philosophy can help theology against atheism, Sadducism or materialism, enthusiasm, and an excessive love of disputation. The section on Sadducism is his most earnest attempt to make this assistance practical. Glanvill writes: "*Philosophy . . . from divers Operations* in our *own Souls* concludes, that there is a sort of Beings which are not Matter or Body." That is, the minimal basis for the truth Scripture teaches about the continued existence of the soul after death and a state of future reward and punishment is provided by philosophy, which, in its analysis of human conduct, finds reason to assert spirituality. Glanvill freely admits that the express words of Scripture and philosophical analysis may, on occasion, disagree, but only because of the generic demands of Scripture, whose authors sometimes use imagery that complies with the infirmities of an unphilosophical audience.[18] Some of the specific, practical alliances Glanvill builds between religion and philosophy are not strong; his governing assumption, that the two are in fundamental agreement, is more significant than his practical instances.

The fifth essay comes to the heart of Anglican rational theology about the truth of Scripture. Glanvill argues that Scripture is true because two fundamental propositions are true: God exists and his authority stands behind Scripture. The first is proved from the beauty and order of creation and the second from the miracles performed by the authors of Scripture. He then divides the formal principles of Christianity into those that are "mixt" and those that are "pure," that is, "those known *only* by Divine Testimony."[19] Reason and revelation reinforce each other in the certification of "mixt" principles such as the attributes of God, the immortality of the soul, and the difference between good and evil; it is significant that Glanvill did not seem to believe that these principles could be enunciated by reason alone, without the influence of revelation. Although the two essays argue strongly for the usefulness of philosophy to apologetics, "pure" Christianity comes from Scripture alone, and philosophy, however often it is invoked, occupies a secondary place in the apologetical structure that houses the Christian religion.

Glanvill's two essays only sketch the guidelines of rational theology after 1660. A more general methodology was needed to reconcile faith and reason, a mode of conceiving them that did not depend on the piecemeal instances of reconciliation that Glanvill provides. A more direct and universal confrontation with Hobbes's and Spinoza's separation of faith and reason had, in fact, been made. As long as theology rested only on faith, in Spinoza's sense, only on an obedient, voluntaristic response to Scripture, no rational theology was possible. Before and after Glanvill wrote, then, the major divines addressed themselves to two general questions: how to make the object of faith somehow commensurate with the object of reason, and how to establish, on the psychological level, a unified mode of conceiving faith and reason as part of the same whole.

The divines' discussion of these issues, especially by Barrow and

Tillotson, occurred over several years, often in sermons that cannot be precisely dated. The following analysis is thus synthetic and relies on a reading of a number of texts from the 1660s and 1670s. These texts offered a simple solution to the first problem.

Hobbes objected to a confusion in language "in the writings of divines," saying that they misconstrued or left ambiguous the meaning of the verb, πιστεύειν, to believe, which properly takes as its formal object a person whose veracity is to be trusted. The statements or propositions enunciated by this person make up a second, and improper, object, although the divines confused the matter by sliding from one meaning to another without adequate warning and distinguishing.[20] Isaac Barrow most clearly responded to this problem. Barrow simply reversed the order of the meanings of the object of πιστεύειν. The object of faith, he wrote, is primarily propositional; πιστεύειν does not mean faith in a person but faith in that person's statements. Propositions always form the primary object of belief.[21]

The truth of theological statements drawn from Scripture may indeed rest on different evidence than the truth of mathematical statements. But truth always occurs in statements, in any field of endeavor, including rational theology. Therefore it is possible for reason to move easily from philosophy to theology because the contents of both, being propositional, are analogous. In the twentieth century, scholars are so inured to personalist philosophy that Barrow's contribution to the theology of faith may seem strange. Barrow, however, did not insist on the propositional nature of faith as a means to attack some protopersonalism existing in the seventeenth century. He adopted such a tactic, as did Stillingfleet and Tillotson, in an attempt to counter the Hobbist premise that, from the point of view of its object, faith will always involve an inferior form of knowledge.

The divines' answer to the second problem, concerning a psychological whole as parts of which both faith and reason can be conceived, is more complex. Stillingfleet stated the common view of faith, which, in the context of the seventeenth-century philosophical critique of scriptural religion, was radical: "By *Faith* we understand a *rational* and *discursive Act* of the Mind. For *Faith* being an *assent* upon *Evidence* or *Reason* inducing the Mind to assent, it must be a *rational* and *discursive* Act" and "a *Perswa-*

sion of the Mind."[22] Faith, in Tillotson's words, is "a Perswasion of the mind concerning any thing; concerning the truth of any Proposition, concerning the Existence, or Futurition, or Lawfulness, or Convenience, or Possibility, or Goodness of any thing, or the contrary." "Faith" includes, then, all operations of the mind, except in its prepropositional stages, an area with which the divines, together with much secular philosophy at this time, were not overly concerned. Apparently no post-propositional activities were excluded from such a conception of faith. Even if some truths are self-evident and may be grasped without discursive activity, they will at length be expressed in propositions, and faith will direct their formulation at that point. "Faith," writes Tillotson, "is not opposed to Error, and Knowledge, and Opinion: but comprehends all these under it."[23]

A complicated substratum of divisions and distinctions under the heading of "faith" allowed the divines to enlarge its meaning so extravagantly. In Tillotson's analysis, from the point of view of cause, the persuasion that is faith can be achieved from sense, from experience, from reason, and from testimony. Conscious that many, including Hobbes and Spinoza, conceived of faith as a human activity based only on the evidence of testimony, the divines did not argue the point but let their more comprehensive analysis stand on its own merits.[24] Each of the four types of argument may cause a faith of various degrees of certainty. In a characteristically English and empirical departure from Descartes, the divines held that arguments from sense cause the highest and firmest degree of faith. Arguments from experience cause a degree of faith of less certainty than sense but more than reason. Arguments from reason vary in degree of certainty. If necessary reasoning is involved, for example, from compelling first principles, faith is firm and certain; if probabilities are involved, a greater or lesser degree of doubt will always accompany the proof. Arguments from testimony depend for their efficacy on the credibility of the person who testifies; if the person is God, who cannot lie, testimony "begets the firmest perswasion, and the highest degree of Faith in its kind." Finally, there are two fundamentally different types of faith from the point of view of its object: civil or human and divine or religious. Religious faith includes, as its objects, the truths of natural religion, supernatural and revealed truths, and the single, important truth that supernatural and revealed truths are in fact based on the authority of God.[25]

One should not conclude from this scheme that the divines, in self-seeking tactics, hid away, in its final recesses, the scientific and philosophical accomplishments of their age, under the heading of civil and humane matters. The major divines were not ignorant of these accomplishments. Barrow, the teacher of Isaac Newton, in the course of homiletic argument compared the relative certainty of his conclusions with those of the "Theorems of any Science."[26] In a work published posthumously, Stillingfleet used data learned from the American voyages of discovery to argue to the common consent of mankind about the existence of God, reinforcing the argument from "universal wisdom" used by Herbert of Cherbury.[27] Also, because scientific propositions form the object of one kind of faith, all four causes of faith may be applied to them in a way not unproductive of insight into their formulation.

The skeptic may complain, somewhat justly from his point of view, that the divines' scheme of faith is lopsided in that it emphasizes specifically religious faith. The divines took a different view. However self-serving their scheme might have been, it attempted a view of the whole, seeking to unite rather than to separate science and theology. It is not brilliant and perhaps not elegant, but it is not ignorant. Reason and revelation—the terms frequently used to discuss the divines' allegiances—remain distinct, but they are distinct inside a structure that allows for intercommunication on common grounds of evidence. Above all, the scheme allowed the divines to pursue their own concern—a rational account of the Christian religion—with clarity. Keeping this scheme in mind, one can construct a continuum of the core doctrines of Christianity without separating them from philosophical truths about the natural world or man.

The Existence of God.

For obvious reasons, the evidence of sense and experience does not normally apply, nor does the argument from certain authority. As Tillotson notes, the testimony of God cannot be used to prove God, and the doctrine of God's existence is too important to depend entirely upon human testimony.[28] The divines relied on two traditional arguments from reason: from the ordered frame of the world and from universal consent. Tillotson adverted to the Cartesian argument from the idea of God to its necessary existence; Stillingfleet explored this argument more fully, accepting it early in his writing career and later finding it wanting.[29]

The Immortality of the Soul.

Although the divines considered traditional proofs from reason, they also based this doctrine on the testimony of Scripture. Barrow, for example, admitted that reason tells us that the soul is immortal but noted the weakness of reason and the necessity that the doctrine also be confirmed by the testimony of Scripture.[30] The possibility of God's self-revelation in Scripture is generally thought to be logically involved with the doctrine of immortality: if we are immortal, then there is a rational necessity that God reveal the means whereby we might live with him forever. Stillingfleet said that "clear and evident" reason leads us to deduce "the necessity of some particular *Divine Revelation*, as the *Standard* and measure of Religion."[31] Because the divines asserted the immortality of the soul on the evidence of both reason and testimony, it is clear that the existence of God was the single doctrine commonly held by late seventeenth-century Anglicans to be based solely on the evidence of reason.

The Divine Authority of the Scriptures.

As a general rule, this doctrine is proved, somewhat circularly, from the testimony of the Scriptures. That the authors of Scripture worked miracles, the argument goes, certifies that they participated in the power and truthfulness of God. Various arguments from reason may also be offered as proof of Scripture's authority, though these tend to be of lesser probability. That Scripture has the power to triumph over opposition or that its plain style inevitably speaks the truth are arguments that occur frequently.

Sacramental and Ecclesiastical Questions.

All arguments are finally based on the evidence of the testimony of Scripture, with occasional help from the testimony of the Fathers of the Church. The divines repeatedly rejected the Roman Catholic doctrine of transubstantiation, that the substance of bread and wine becomes the substance of the body and blood of Christ in the Holy Communion. The negative evidence against transubstantiation comes from an absence of scriptural testimony and the doctrine's violation of the evidence of sense. The divines were especially concerned that acceptance of any doctrine that violates the senses may reflect on the sense-evidence given by the first Christians about miracles. If sense cannot be trusted in one area, can it be in another?

The Christian Mysteries.

All firm persuasion of the Trinity and Incarnation, and the few other central mysteries, is necessarily based on the testimony of Scripture. Their probation is, in a sense, what Scripture exists for. The divines were anxious to prove, however, that once these mysteries are revealed to exist, they may be shown, on the evidence of reason, to be possible. Reason finds their existence plausible but cannot enter into the manner of their existence. Such mysteries are above reason, therefore, but not against it.

III

With this scheme of faith and short catalog of doctrinal evidences in mind, it is possible to proceed to the difficult analysis of what the Anglican divines of the later seventeenth century meant by "reason" and how their definition of it may be distinguished from its definition in other intellectual movements of their day. First, when the divines spoke of reason they did not usually mean it in the sense of the reason or "right reason" of the Cambridge Platonists. For the seventeenth-century English Platonists, reason is an elevated faculty, which, in its operations and in contact with innate ideas, participates in divine reason. Moreover, this participation occurs in the context of a devout and contemplative life.[32] Although this sense of reason is profound and far more explicitly connected with Christian living than the reason of the later divines, theology written in the light of it tends to be hermetic. One suspects that the divines considered it of limited apologetical use. They frequently noted that an evil life would cloud the mind in its attempts to perceive divine truth. Their positive appreciation of the connection between right reason and Christian living, however, was not highly developed. The integration of doctrine and life evident in the writings of the Cambridge Platonists seemed foreign to the divines, who liked to think their theological project would persuade any unbiased, though not necessarily pious, person.

In trying to understand what the divines meant by reason, rational proof, and the rational grounds for Christianity, we may distinguish between a narrower and a wider sense of reason. Reason in the narrow sense is the reason of philosophy that operates strictly on its own first principles. Reason in this sense analyzes human nature and the physical world; conclusions from this analysis are then brought to bear, if at all, upon theological questions. Reason in this sense also gives evidence for truth, theological or otherwise, by comparing the internal content of this truth with the perceived necessary laws of the mind, such as the principle of contradiction, the principle that certain things cannot exist without attendant conditions, or the principle that truth occurs only in clear and distinct ideas. The universal consent of mankind or, especially in England, the evidence of the senses may also be used to establish the truth of a proposition. Reason in this narrow sense, however, resists evidence from testimony, human or divine. Although the divines always were cognizant of divine testimony, they employed reason in the narrow sense when proving the existence of God from an idea of God that necessarily implies its own existence. Further uses are not difficult to isolate, even in discussions of the Trinity, which is shown, though after its revelation is accepted, to be not contradictory to such necessary doctrine as the existence of one God. Finally, reason in the narrow sense claims to possess something like mathematical certainty in regard to its conclusions.

Reason in a wider sense is reason that is informed not only by its own laws but by the matter it is investigating. In the context of the rational theology of the later seventeenth century, this definition means that reason is disposed toward a full acceptance of the full contents of Scripture. Reason in this sense, as in Tillotson's scheme, refers both to persuasion caused by the evidence of reason in a narrow sense and to the fuller and more comprehensive operations of the mind that result in persuasion by any of the four types of evidence. This wider sense tolerates less strict proofs based on probabilities, particularly proofs based on testimony. Although reason in this sense still presents logically ordered proofs, it does not maintain that these proofs possess mathematical certainty. Reason in this sense attempts to present probabilities that believing Christians may use to buttress their belief and from which unprejudiced individuals will find it difficult to hold back their assent.

All the writers I have discussed in this chapter—both the divines and the philosophers who divorced reason and faith—employed reason in both these senses. The distinction between the divines and the philosophers involves matters of stress and emphasis. For the divines, reason in a narrow sense is a secondary operation after the truth of Scripture as a whole is otherwise authenticated; this is not so for Spinoza and Toland. Considering its own structure inviolable, reason in a narrow sense either refuses to admit rationally untidy doctrine as part of scriptural revelation or rationalizes such doctrine out of the sense in which tradition has held it to exist. Reason in a wider sense never reads Scripture, in Toland's words, with the same rules "from what is common to all other Books." If Scripture is held to be both clear statement of doctrine and divine testimony, then reason must, from the beginning of its inquiry, assure that it leaves a place in its operations for accepting such testimony. Indeed, this need of assurance of a place for Scripture seems to motivate the comprehensiveness of Tillotson's attempt to set up the categories of faith as a persuasion of different types of truth by different evidences.

We may ask whether reason in this wider sense avoids the issue of Hobbes's and Spinoza's distinction between faith and knowledge. For it does admit, as a constituent object of rational inquiry, the possible existence of an external principle that guarantees Scripture's truth irrespective of its rational content, a principle potentially irreducible to rational laws. At the very least, this principle guarantees the truth of the manner of existence of the central scriptural mysteries, which is admittedly not understandable by reason in any sense. Reason in this wider sense thus holds, in its core, an abiding affection for a source of truth that is not rationally verifiable in all its operations; such a commitment is not the result of a persuasion but of some deeper human act that has always been called, in spite of the divines' attempt to broaden the category, specifically religious faith.

The divines did not leave the concept of divine testimony without rational underpinnings. But reason in a narrow sense asserts only that if God reveals himself, given the nature of God, his self-revelation must be true; reason in a wider sense establishes that this or that book or passage of Scripture does in fact instance divine revelation. We must admit that, if the divines consciously faced their own departure from the reason of the philosophers, they did not candidly communicate this awareness. Such coyness about fundamental methodology has made historical inquiry into their thought a difficult task; the divines' reticence in speaking of their prerational bias has encouraged subsequent use of the term "rationalism" to describe their project. Yet their theology, which has at its heart commitment to mystery that is irreducible to rational notions, scarcely fulfills the basic requirements of the category.

The divines' methodology, employing reason in both a narrow and a wide sense, was worked out in hundreds of sets of proofs between 1660 and 1700. Two of these many proofs provide a sample of the practical application of the theoretical scheme of rational faith and are representative, I think, of the entire project: Tillotson's proof of the unchangeableness of God and Stillingfleet's of the satisfaction paid by Jesus for sin. These two proofs rest on different first principles. Reason in a narrow sense establishes the unchangeability of God as a truth consequent on his existence; explicitly scriptural revelation establishes the doctrine of the satisfaction of Jesus. Yet in Tillotson's and Stillingfleet's discussions of these doctrines, there is no great difference in the reasoning used to prove their truth.

Tillotson's *Several Discourses upon the Attributes of God*, volume 6 of his posthumously collected works, contains eleven sermons that prove the perfection, happiness, unchangeableness, knowledge, wisdom, justice, truth, and holiness of God. Any of these sermons would illustrate the application of the two types of reason I have discussed; that on God's unchangeableness does so in a somewhat more self-conscious way than the others. After a brief explication of the text (James 1 : 17) and an explanation of the term "unchangeableness," Tillotson writes that he intends to prove that "this *Perfection* is essential to God" both "from Natural Reason and from the Divine Revelation of the Holy Scriptures." Showing first that the concept of inconstancy implies weakness and imperfection and that, if God has such qualities, his other perfections and all religion are vitiated, Tillotson concludes the first part of his argument: "This Reasoning is not the result of *Divine Revelation*, but is clearly founded in the *natural* Notions and Suggestions of our Minds."[33] For confirmation, he quotes the pagan philosophers Plato and Seneca, who held this doctrine without benefit of scriptural revelation.

After thus calling attention to the internal rationality of the doctrine, Tillotson enters into its confirmation by Scripture, the second part of the proof. The doctrine will "yet more clearly appear," he writes, "from the Divine Revelation of the Holy Scriptures, which tell us that God is *unchangeable* in his Nature and in his Perfections, in all his Decrees and Purposes and Promises."[34] Tillotson then amasses sixteen short quotations about the unchangeableness of God from Exodus, Numbers, the Psalms, Isaiah, Matthew, Romans, 1 Timothy, and Hebrews. We may ask what is the precise relationship between this display and what has gone before from the stance of "Natural Reason." Could either proof, for example, from reason or Scripture, stand on its own? The brief though complete treatment suggests that each could stand on its own. Tillotson's greater emphasis on his ability to prove the doctrine from reason implies that this proof involves some special distinction. Perhaps he was attempting to show that Scripture is unnecessary in this matter; yet the weight of his alternate proof, from Scripture, and the tenor of his theological work do not lend credibility to the idea that he would want to deemphasize or downgrade Scripture. It is more likely that he had in mind an opponent such as Spinoza, who had cast doubt on the reasonableness of scriptural doctrine, or at least on the possibility of applying reason to it. Thus Tillotson's treatment makes several points: the truth of the doctrine of God's unchangeableness, the presence of this doctrine both in the findings of reason and in Scripture, and the further point that a self-conscious operation of reason in a narrow sense perfectly aligns with and substantiates what one finds in Scripture.

Stillingfleet's discussion of the satisfaction paid by Jesus for sin occurs in an early anti-Socinian work, *A Discourse Concerning the Sufferings of Christ* (1668–69), which he republished in 1696. Chapter 2 of this work establishes that the doctrine of Jesus' satisfaction for sin rests on the literal sense of Scripture. Chapter 3, our concern here, attempts to show more explicitly how the doctrine is reasonable. Stillingfleet writes: "We come now to debate the matter in point of reason. And if there appear nothing repugnant in the nature of the thing, or to the justice of God, then all their [the Socinians'] loud clamours will come to nothing; for on that they fix, when they talk the most of our Doctrine being contrary to reason."[35] Stillingfleet cultivates here a studied ambiguity in regard to the "point of reason." He does not say, as he might of other doctrines, that reason compels us to accept this doctrine; rather, calling it "our Doctrine," he hints that a predisposition to accept it exists and that the human mind may be satisfied if nothing found by reason prevents its acceptance.

Both Stillingfleet and the Socinians accepted the scriptural fact that Jesus suffered. Their differences concern the motives and conditions for this fact. After some pages of discussion of the possibility of freely vicarious suffering for the sins of others as evidenced by a number of scriptural texts, here used as true statements about the human condition, Stillingfleet continues:

I now return to the *consent of Mankind* in it, on supposition either of a near conjunction, or a valid consent which must make up the want of dominion in men without it. And the question still proceeds upon the supposition of those things, that there be a proper dominion in men over that which they part with for others sakes, and that they do it by their free consent; and then we justifie it not to be repugnant to the principles of Reason and Justice, for any to suffer beyond the *desert* of their actions.[36]

In other words, as did Tillotson on the unchangeableness of God, Stillingfleet adds the evidence of reason in a narrower sense, of "the consent of Mankind" and of "the principles of Reason and Justice," to the evidence of Scripture, on the possibility of an individual's free assumption of the punishment owed to others. Again the structure of the proof makes points about both doctrine and methodology: the doctrine of Jesus' satisfaction is true, and there is no reason to suspect that Scripture's avowal of it is irrational. For the more narrow evidence of common consent and rational principle supports the testimony of the Old and New Testaments. In this instance, of course, the rational evidence cannot stand alone; for reason by itself could not have enunciated this doctrine. Granted that impossibility and once Scripture establishes the doctrine, the believer may also find narrower rational grounds to stand on.

The interplay here of various senses of reason is complex. If revelation rationally proved to be from God did not proclaim the doctrine, there would be no need to search for its grounds in universal consent; reason in a wider sense thus conditions the narrower sense and brings to fruition its latent possibilities as a source of proof. In both these proofs of Tillotson and Stillingfleet, concerning religious truths resting on different first principles, we catch the same free but self-conscious interplay of different kinds of rational probation. The divisions of the proofs clearly respect the autonomy of the different senses of reason; yet the wholes made of these proofs show how, in the act of rational theologizing, philosophy and theology are not opposed, as Spinoza said, but complementary.

IV

Much of the Old Testament, written in the genre of historical narrative, does not easily lend itself to abstract, dogmatic formulation. If there is one constant pattern or doctrine taught by the historical Scripture, it would seem to be the simple one of conversion, idolatry, and reconversion. Such a pattern, if of great homiletic value, scarcely helped the divines of the late seventeenth century prove the rational truth of the historical Scripture, an essential part of their project. It would seem that they could have done so by comparative history, showing how scriptural history holds a more reliable view of the facts than secular history; by hypothesizing how things must have been and showing how Scripture accords with the hypothesis; and by showing that an external source proves that scriptural history is true, the proof from authority. All these methodologies were current in England between 1660 and 1700.

A major instance of an attempt at comparative history occurs in the first two books of Stillingfleet's compendious *Origines Sacrae* (1662), the first major theological book of the Restoration. The first book castigates the falsity, self-interest, and faulty chronology of "heathen" histories of cosmic origins; the second praises the truth of the Old Testament records. The first book argues "that there is no ground of credibility in the account of ancient times given by any Heathen Nations different from the Scriptures, which I have with much care and diligence inquired into." [37] Later Stillingfleet writes, "I shall *demonstrate . . . that there is no ground of assent to any ancient histories which give an account of things different from the Scriptures, from these arguments; the apparent defect, weakness, and insufficiency* of them as to the giving an account of elder times; *The monstrous confusion, ambiguity, and uncertainty* of them in the account which they give: the *evident partiality* of them to themselves, and *inconsistency with each other.*" [38] There follow six chapters filled with enumerations of these defects in Phoenician, Egyptian, Chaldean, and Greek history. The language of Stillingfleet's announcements of his project implies that reason in a narrow sense will be applied to historical records. His treatment of his first objection, however, the defect and insufficiency of heathen records, shows that this is not to be the case. Stillingfleet complains that "any certain way of *preserving tradition* is wanting" in the heathen cultures, that the antiquity of their certain records is doubtful, and that oral communication previous to records is necessarily uncertain: "*Words* being of so *perishing* a *nature*, and mans *memory*, so *weak* and *frail* in retaining them, it is *necessary* for a *certain communication* of *knowledge*, that some *way* should be found out more *lasting* than *words*, more *firm* than memory and more *faithful* than *tradition.*" [39] The argument seems reasonable in the context of the first book. But Stillingfleet is not without the "evident partiality" of which he accuses his heathen subjects. It is understandable that he should have the written Mosaic records in mind at this point; in the background one also catches sight of a Roman Catholic apologist, who claims the necessity of nonwritten tradition to explain Scripture. The whole of the author's scriptural apologetics informs his discussion of heathen records; he writes of prehistory in such a way that its lessons may also serve to counter seventeenth-century theological adversaries. A rational methodology that proclaims its impartiality turns out to be one guided, in its arguments, by sectarian debates among Christian denominations.

The first book of *Origines Sacrae* exhibits impressive familiarity with the contents of heathen records. The thirty-two-year-old apologist shows himself an adept researcher of both original records and previous Renaissance compilations of Phoenician, Egyptian, Chaldean, and Greek accounts. At one point, however, Stillingfleet suddenly shifts his point of view from that of the rational, comparative historian. The Greek historians, he writes, try to give an account of the origin of nations, even though they do not know

the *state* of those *Nations* which they pretend to give an account of. For where there is wanting *divine revelation* (which was not pretended by any Greek historians; and if it had, had been easily refuted) there must be supposed a full and exact knowledge of all things pertaining to that which they pretend to give an account of; and if they discover apparent *defect* and *insufficiency* (which hath been largely manifested as to them, in the precedent discourse) we have ground to deny the *credibility* of those *histories* upon the account of such defect and insufficiency.[40]

In other words, in judging the truth of primitive historical records, two different criteria present themselves: one regarding content and another the author, who may or may not write in the context of divine revelation. The heathen records are judged deficient in the first case; the second possibility does not pertain to them. The Hebrew records, which Stillingfleet discusses in book 2 of *Origines Sacrae*, are judged from the point of view of their author as a divinely inspired writer. Nowhere in the book does Stillingfleet criticize the content of the Hebrew primitive records. Stillingfleet's attempt at comparative history does not seem to be strictly comparative, for the internal verification of one set of records is balanced against the external verification of others.

In the 1680s and 1690s the work of Thomas Burnet, in *The Sacred*

Theory of the Earth (1684 and 1690) and *Archaeologiae Philosophicae* (1692), attempted a more rationalistic interpretation of parts of the Mosaic history. Burnet proposed to reconcile natural philosophy with four instances of scriptural history: the deluge, the garden of Eden, the final conflagration, and the new heavens and earth. One may gain an insight into his methodology by examining his first and most well-known defense of scriptural history, that of the deluge. Burnet accepts the basic truth of the Mosaic account although acknowledging that it presents problems from the point of view of natural philosophy. He is especially bothered by the source of the waters of the deluge; given the shape of the earth as we know it, neither a downpour of forty days and nights nor water from any other natural source could totally cover the earth: "We have left no corner unsought, where there was any appearance of a report of water to be found, and yet we have not been able to collect the eighth part of what was necessary upon a moderate account. May we not then with assurance include, that the world hath taken the wrong measures hitherto in their notion and explication of the general deluge?"[41] On the basis of a few passages from the Psalms and from the New Testament, especially 2 Peter 3 : 5–7 ("the world that then was being overflowed with water"), and reason, working somewhat autonomously, Burnet proposed to seek a scientific explanation inside nature for the abundance of waters, rather than to assent to their miraculous appearance, as the literal sense of Scripture seems to teach. He postulates that before the deluge, the earth took the shape of a smooth and hollow ball—a form more rationally and aesthetically convenient to a divine creation and also one with less area than the imperfect world as we now know it. At the time of the deluge, the shell of the spherical earth cracked, allowing waters hidden in its interior to surge up and flood the earth.[42]

In elaborating this fantastic theory, Burnet used Scripture as a source of historical truth in a curious way. He took physical descriptions of the earth given in the Psalms literally; Scripture clearly gives evidence for his theory of the earth of equal authority with that of reason. Yet he had to face the basic difficulty that the Mosaic account does not specifically teach the spherical smoothness of the antediluvian earth. To solve this difficulty and to preserve the inspired integrity of Moses, he insisted that Moses wrote as he did, though knowing the alternate truth, only because

the vulgar mass was incapable of understanding philosophy. Moses' account, he writes, "bears in it evident marks of an accommodation and
condescension to the vulgar notions concerning the form of the World."[43]
In Genesis, Moses wished "to expound the first Originals of Things after
such a Method, as might breed in the Minds of Men Piety and a Worship-
ping of the true God"; he hid the truth because his audience, being an
"ignorant people," could not have understood it.[44] Much in Burnet's argument is reminiscent of Spinoza's *Tractatus*, but, in its allowance that
Genesis teaches, even in disguised fashion, a true theory of the earth, the
argument is clearly not Spinozan.

Burnet's reinterpretation of Mosaic history caused a number of more
traditionally minded divines and laymen to respond, though none of
them are major figures. Burnet, writes Herbert Croft, bishop of Here-
ford, "allows no Miracle in the Deluge, but will needs have all done by
Intelligible and Rational ways"; many passages "he hath wrested from
their own plain and easie understanding; obscuring all, and forcing from
them a most remote and difficult sense."[45] Even John Beaumont, a friendly
critic, objected that one need not bend over backward to rationalize
Scripture to please atheists and that Burnet's theory of the deluge, in spite
of its attempts to make the scriptural occurrence more rationally accept-
able, made it more complicated than it was.[46]

Burnet's reconciliation of Scripture and natural history is important
less for the fanciful conclusions it draws than for the rules for reading
scriptural history on which it depends. He attempted to occupy a middle
ground between Spinoza and the divines. The literal sense of Scripture
does not, at least in Genesis, teach natural philosophy, but if we read be-
low the surface—in a way not easily corresponding to any of the four traditional readings of Scripture—we can find its truth about natural phenomena. Burnet shared the divines' respect for the integrity of Scripture
but could do so only by a nonliteral reading. Indeed, a literal reading
might encourage nonbelief. The "vulgar style of Scripture," he writes,
"hath often been mistaken for the real sence, and so becomes a stumbling
block in the way of truth"; "when nature and reason will bear a literal
sense, the rule is that we should not recede from the letter."[47]

Still, in matters of natural philosophy, the literal sense of Scripture
cannot be the final word. "Scripture never undertook, nor was ever de-

signed to teach us Philosophy and the Arts and Sciences," and "it is of no fault to recede from the literal sence of Scripture, but the fault is when we leave it without a just cause."[48] Burnet's writings reveal some inconsistency on this point: he insists on the literal sense of the Psalms and the New Testament when they support his theory but not on the literal sense of Genesis when it does not. Or perhaps natural philosophy is the determining factor in choosing whether one looks for the literal or nonliteral sense of a passage. Only when the literal sense supports natural philosophy can it be received wholeheartedly. "There is a great difference between Scripture with Philosophy on its side," Burnet elusively writes, "and Scripture with Philosophy against it: when the question is concerning the Natural World."[49]

The attempts by Burnet and Stillingfleet to rationalize scriptural history show the limits of bringing forth internal evidence to prove that the history which Scripture narrates is in fact true. Stillingfleet applied reason in a narrow sense to heathen records but not to the Mosaic history; Burnet applied reason only to the data about the natural world found in that account. Neither could resolve the methodological conflict between divine testimony and natural philosophy; both finally had to give in to one side of the conflict in order to provide a coherent account of cosmic origins. It is clear that a rational defense of the whole of scriptural history on the basis of internal evidence was a difficult and perhaps impossible task, especially in an age of scientific revolution, when self-conscious attention to correct methodology had moved to the forefront of scholarly inquiry.

In spite of Stillingfleet's attempts to reconcile scriptural history and critical methodology in the first book of *Origines Sacrae*, he and his fellow Anglican divines seemed aware that the project would not be fruitful. They knew that to examine each historical account, and even each doctrine in Scripture, and to attempt to prove all true on internal evidence were impossible. To supplement their inquiries in this area, the divines worked hard at establishing verifying principles for the truth of Scripture based on an external principle of authority, the proof from divine testimony.

3

Testimony and Other Arguments:
Miracles and the Integration of Proofs

$\mathbb{P}$ost-Enlightenment students of the later seventeenth century have often read their own evidentiary concerns back into the writings of the Anglican theologians of that period; the balance of understanding has often been tipped in the direction of the evidence of reason, in a narrow sense, as a proof for the truth of Scripture. In fact, the divines placed the weight of their argumentation for such truth elsewhere. If they stressed one type of evidence in Tillotson's scheme of faith to the point of unbalance, it was the evidence of and argument from testimony. This argument depends, as Tillotson wrote, on the credibility of the witnesses giving testimony. If those witnesses bear the marks of divine authority, their testimony is undoubtedly true. It is clear that they possess such authority if they have accomplished miracles, violations of nature which only God can cause. When Robert South asked why the doctrine of Jesus Christ is true, he allowed that the excellency of its contents and the agreement of Jesus' life with the prophecies of the Old Testament could be argued. But Jesus' miracles alone are "undoubtedly high proofs": they "were the syllogisms of heaven, and the argumentations of Omnipotence."[1] Tillotson agreed: "In Reason, Miracles are the highest Attestation that can be given to the Truth and Divinity of any Doctrine."[2] South, Tillotson, and others warned that the content of any doctrine proved by miracles must be examined; South said, for example, that miracles can never be forwarded to prove a doctrine contrary to the commandments.[3] Nevertheless, within these strictures, the divines did not habitually claim that the doctrines of Scripture are internally self-verifying; a rational account of its external source in a person who worked miracles would be its highest verification.

The divines of the later seventeenth century did not invent the argument from miracles. On the one hand, the argument makes explicit in doctrinal form the many accounts in Scripture in which a hostile audience begins to believe an individual prophet such as Moses or Jesus because of the miracles he performs. On the other, the argument from miracles makes its appearance in other seventeenth-century contexts. Spinoza attacked miracles in chapter 6 of the *Tractatus* partly because of the use he knew was made of them to prove the divine authority of Scripture. In 1638, William Chillingworth adverted to miracles as a proof that Scripture is God's word.[4] He did not develop the argument, presumably because Roman Catholics, his stated adversaries, were regarded throughout the century as overly credulous about miracles. The Cambridge Platonists Ralph Cudworth and Henry More both mentioned miracles only to warn their readers to be wary of an argument based on them.[5] The confidence of the Cambridge Platonists in human reason as a participation in the divine mind did not encourage them to seek such external proofs for Scripture's authority. The major Anglican divines of the late seventeenth century, taking as their province the full analysis of a wider range of proofs, became enthusiastic defenders of the proof for authority they inherited.

The case for the argument from testimony rests most strongly on the major miracle-workers of Scripture and the books commonly associated with them: Moses and the Pentateuch; the prophets; Jesus himself in the Gospels; and the apostles and disciples whose miracles are recorded in Acts and who are proximately or remotely responsible for the books of the New Testament which bear their names. Books of the Old Testament of uncertain authorship, or by an author not recorded as a miracle-worker, become authoritative, according to the argument, through their implicit acceptance or explicit quotation by Jesus or a New Testament author. A disruption of the laws of nature, as evident in a true miracle, can occur only through the intervention of the creator of those laws, God himself.

When God permits such a disruption, he places a seal of approval on the human person historically responsible; God makes him thereby a credible spokesman for himself. God involves his own authority when he allows the sudden alterations of physical nature, the healings, and the resurrections that punctuate the Old and New Testaments. As John Wilkins, bishop of Chester, wrote in 1675, "'Tis not consistent with the nature of the Deity, his Truth, Wisdom, or Justice, to work such miracles in confirmation of a Lye or Imposture."[6]

It would be a possible though unwieldy task to show how each of the major authors of Scripture was certified and rendered authoritative by one or another of the divines. We may confine ourselves to looking at the greatest of these authorial inquisitions published in the later seventeenth century, Edward Stillingfleet's analysis of the Mosaic authorship in *Origines Sacrae* (1662). The Mosaic authorship had begun to be a controversial issue by midcentury. The usual critics in opposition, Hobbes and Spinoza, did not accept the traditional ascription of the first five books of Scripture to Moses, at least not in their entirety. At the very least, they argued, Moses did not write the account of his death or accounts of events that happened after his death.[7]

In his treatment of the Mosaic authorship, Stillingfleet tried to prove the matter in general and did not get bogged down in the problems involved with this or that verse. He began by establishing, from external evidence, that Moses wrote that which is traditionally assigned to him. Such evidence includes the universal consent of Jews and Gentiles that Moses wrote the Jewish Law on which a commonwealth was founded. It is very clear from the whole of the Old Testament that the Jews at times felt the Law to be a burden. If it were at all possible, would not the Jews have aired any suspicions that the Law was not Moses' as an excuse for avoiding its observance? Stillingfleet did not pretend that these arguments, based on probabilities, would satisfy the hostile critic. He explicitly stated that, throughout his argument for Moses' authorship of the Pentateuch, he could only attempt to evoke "moral certainty," which, nevertheless, is "a *sufficient foundation* for an *undoubted assent*" based on arguments "strong enough to convince an unbiased mind."[8] It is interesting that precisely in the context of the Mosaic authorship Spinoza uttered a dictum that presumes a methodology directly contrary to Stillingfleet's argument: "We must not accept what is reasonably probable."[9]

Citing two New Testament passages (Acts 7:21 and Hebrews 11:25) about Moses' education at the court in Egypt, Stillingfleet wrote a substantial essay on the powers of Egyptian learning and culture. Moses' acquaintance with these accounts for the encyclopedic lore evident in the Pentateuch. Although Stillingfleet's treatment borders on the fanciful, his intention is clear enough: he wants to account for Moses' education rationally and historically, rather than to ascribe it, in some fundamentalist way, to directly divine intervention. Moses' learning thus historically accounted for, Stillingfleet examines the "fidelity" and "integrity" of his character. Because Moses "hath so interwoven the *History* of his own *failings* and *disobedience* with those of the Nation," his authorship can hardly be thought to be self-serving. He writes with "*innate simplicity* and *plainness*," which shows that he "thought that *Truth* it self had presence enough with it, to *command* the *submission* of our *understandings* to it." The final proof of Moses' integrity—and of the truth of his writings—is "the *rational Evidence* of that divine authority whereby *Moses* acted, which may be gathered from that *divine power* which appeared in *his actions*," that is, his miracles.[10]

In his analysis of the Mosaic authorship, Stillingfleet established a four-part model, which appeared from 1662 on, in whole or in part, as the foundation for the argument from testimony to the truth of Scripture:

(1) A confirmation that the traditional author wrote the book assigned to him; the divines usually employed the argument from universal consent to do this.

(2) An analysis of the audience of the book and the speeches recorded in it: that these often converted audiences against their superficial self-interest stands as a proof for the divine authority of the writer. An attempt is also made to provide pagan witnesses to the power of the events narrated in the book who, though not converted by this power, stood in awe and respect of its human agent.

(3) A discussion of the character and style of the author: a plain style is taken as a mark of its truth, as an elaborate style would be a mark of insincerity. The divines allowed their own aesthetic preference for the

plain style to determine what they looked for as authoritative in and of Scripture itself.

(4) Notice of the miracles performed by the author: these are the final proof of his divine authority and the book's truth. Stillingfleet carefully called this final evidence "rational." Although such evidence is in fact superrational, in that it breaks the laws of nature which reason by itself perceives, the evidence is also rational in that it offers substantial proof of the presence of the only power which reason can find capable of breaking those laws.

When Anglicans relied on such a model as Stillingfleet proposed, they did not argue that Moses wrote every single word of the Pentateuch as we now know it, or King David of the Psalms, or Paul of the writings attributed to him. As Thomas Tenison, future archbishop of Canterbury, wrote, specifically against Hobbes, if some of the parts of the Pentateuch were not written by Moses, this does not necessarily detract from the truth of the whole.[11] The question of the Mosaic authorship was hotly debated, especially in the 1680s and 1690s, after the publication of the work of Richard Simon on the Pentateuch; Simon showed that the Pentateuch could not be singly authored. I shall discuss in Chapter 5 the larger issues Simon raised for Anglicans; here it is important that two authors of the mid-1690s tried to combine the older view of the Mosaic authorship, as enunciated by Stillingfleet, with the newer empirical proofs that the Pentateuch could not have been the work of one author.

A comparison of the work of Richard Kidder, bishop of Bath and Wells, and Jean LeClerc, a Swiss liberal theologian living in Holland, provides insight into the Anglican way of dealing with allegedly non-Mosaic parts of the Pentateuch. Both Kidder and LeClerc wrote defenses of the Mosaic authorship by way of examining and defending texts isolated by Hobbes, Spinoza, and others as non-Mosaic; both discussed many of the same texts and used similar arguments. For example, both argued that other ancient texts refer to their authors in the third person and that Moses had intended to write not *annales* but a more concisely theological history.[12]

Kidder was much more reluctant than LeClerc to believe that any individual text discussed was from a non-Mosaic source. Even though Kidder admits in principle that Moses did not write every word of the Pentateuch, of the twenty-two passages he treats, he admits only that Moses may not have written the account of his death in Deuteronomy 34; moreover, he admits this after a discussion of how Moses might have written it.[13] Kidder uses a wide variety of arguments to establish Mosaic authorship of these twenty-two passages: common sense; a close estimate of the Hebrew text, of the literal meaning of the translation, of chronology, and of Moses' intentions; the charge of logical inconsistency against his opponents; and, in a few instances, Moses' prophetic foreknowledge of events. In discussing eighteen disputed passages, LeClerc attributes verses in the Pentateuch to non-Mosaic sources with greater freedom; he also denies the possibility of prophetic foreknowledge which Kidder affirms.[14]

The differences between Kidder and LeClerc are subtle. In the mainstream of Anglican orthodoxy on Scripture, Kidder stresses that Moses is the "Author of these Books"; it is typical of LeClerc's treatment that he relies on the different formula that "the greatest part by far of the *Pentateuch* was written by Moses" and that "almost all of the *Pentateuch* belongs to *Moses*."[15] Kidder candidly asserts his assumption that the burden of argument against Moses' authorship rests on its proponents, whose eccentricity conflicts with the universal testimony of history; he fights these opponents in every instance. More casual and less nervous about the absolute authenticity of every text, LeClerc admits some worth in his opponents' arguments.

In Kidder, one catches sight of a recurring subliminal image in the writings of the Restoration divines: the physical Bible as an icon of devotion. The least detraction from its integrity was heatedly debated, even while the admission was made, perhaps inconsistently, that the whole may not, in all its detail, represent the exact intention of the artist. It is significant that Kidder does not discuss the obvious question which LeClerc brings up: if not Moses, who wrote the disputed passages?[16] Anglicans did not want to bring believers onto the grounds of discussion of non-Mosaic authorship. For both Kidder and LeClerc, the truth of the Bible is connected with the miracles of Moses and other principal authors. LeClerc, however, allows himself to be more speculative about the proof and the evidence against it; he illuminates, by contrast, the rigor with which Anglicans rejected the least textual evidence dissociating the Pentateuch from Moses.[17]

II

In its classical expression in Stillingfleet, the argument from testimony depends on a crowd of improbabilities that individually may be reasonably entertained but, piled one on top of another, seem steeped in credulity. Stillingfleet and others, however, were aware that this proof presented special problems. This awareness accounts for the repeated, nervous insistence, immediately attached to discussion of the proof, that it offers moral certainty only. For the divines, moral certainty, based on moral evidence, first implies a distinction from other kinds of evidence, such as sense or necessary reason. Proofs based on sense and necessary reason compel assent from the sane inquirer, whereas moral evidence, while giving reasonable assurance, cannot remove all doubt. Second, moral certainty has a special relation to "matters of fact," such as are meant when trying to prove the existence of Moses and his miracles. The divines often said that there is as much assurance of the existence and authorship of Moses as of, say, Thucydides and Euclid. One cannot prove historical fact as one can prove certain theorems in geometry; but traditional biblical authorships afford as much certainty as we can have of any historical matters of fact. Last, moral certainty involves the moral nature of the assenting believer. Because moral evidence is not compelling, it demands a free response, for the presence or absence of which the human subject may be held personally accountable. "Moral arguments," writes Tillotson, cannot be "of necessary and infallible efficacy, because they are always propounded to a free Agent who may choose whether he will yield to them or not."[18] Thus the assent to the proof from testimony, from the point of view of moral certainty, offers a paradigm for all human experience of rational faith: enough evidence is available to foster assent, but in such a way that human freedom and accountability retain their integrity.

Even among some Anglican writers of the period moral argumentation was suspect. Samuel Parker, bishop of Oxford during James II's brief reign, did not find moral certainty a meaningful category and preferred instead to emphasize the weight of internal and external arguments for proving the truth of Scripture: "The accumulation of all together amounts to a full evidence of demonstrative certainty."[19] Although Parker's treatment implies a difference of emphasis rather than substance from the thought of Stillingfleet and Tillotson, his note of anxiety is an interesting gloss on their patent enthusiasm for the proof from testimony and miracles. Sir Charles Wolseley, a prominent lay theologian, stressed more than most apologists the necessity for right reason to accompany the presence of miracles in any proof.[20] Together with the qualifications of the major divines, even of Stillingfleet in the later chapters of *Origines Sacrae*, the doubts of Parker and Wolseley in the 1670s and 1680s lead one to sense that the argument from testimony, in spite of the enthusiasm shown for it, was not counted among the purest and most unambiguous riches of Anglican theology. Roman Catholic piety, with a predilection for miracles, in part explains the divines' wariness of any proof involving them. The divines also seemed to sense some internal inadequacy which prevented its presentation from being entirely straightforward.

One of the great conundrums of Anglican scriptural interpretation in this period concerns the proof at issue. For the proof is hopelessly circular. The goal of the proof was to affirm the truth of at least the central books of Scripture. Yet the entire burden of the proof—the character of an author, his reputation, and his miracles—can be found only in the apposite book, whose very truthfulness cannot yet be assumed. It is unreal that such an admirable intellect as Stillingfleet's should fail to see that the truth of Moses' writing, for example, was finally being proved by Moses' writing. In other contexts, the divines showed themselves adept at detecting and avoiding circular proofs. They saw clearly that the existence of God must be shown on nonscriptural grounds before his revelation in Scripture could be discussed. Likewise, in an early anti-Roman argument, Tillotson faulted Roman Catholics for trying to prove the "Divine Authority of the Scripture from the Church, and the Infallibility of the Church back again from Scripture."[21] Even long before the Restoration, Chillingworth had noted the "Circle" of Roman argument concerning a church's protection of an incorrupt text.[22] But I am unable to find a major or minor divine willing to examine the circularity of the proof from testimony.

The one clear critique of the circularity of the proof from testimony that I have found occurs outside the circle of divines of the Restoration establishment. In 1659, immediately before the return of the king, an eminent Puritan writer, John Owen, explicitly rejected miracles as an argument for scriptural authority, on the grounds that miracles are found only in Scripture itself.[23] Even in the short, tight time scheme of so many late seventeenth-century controversies, there was just enough time between Owen's critique and the two earliest manuals of apologetics after 1660—Stillingfleet's *Origines Sacrae* in 1662 and Tillotson's *Rule of Faith* in 1666—for it to be conveniently forgotten. As the parliamentary choice for dean of Christ Church in the Interregnum and a favored preacher of Oliver Cromwell and Sir Thomas Fairfax, Owen was a prominent and controversial churchman. Because of his opposition to the royalism of Westminster School and his attempts at conformity at Christ Church, he made a lifelong enemy of Robert South, a student at both during Owen's ascendancy.[24] In 1680, Owen and Stillingfleet publicly argued about conformity.[25] Whether South or Stillingfleet had read Owen's 1659 work is not known. The general argument of the book—that Scripture, as light and power, eventually validates itself—would cause no rush of either affirmation or negation in the more rationally oriented divines.

The one part of Stillingfleet's model for truth from authority which may address the objection of circularity is the second part: that pagan and even hostile witnesses testify to the character and miracles of the scriptural authors. Yet such testimonials, even as Stillingfleet lists them, are ambiguous and never exactly to the point. Reference to such testimonials makes sense only in the context of the entire argument; they are too frail to stand alone. Why, then, did the major divines hang on so tenaciously to the proof from authority? There are, I think, three answers. First, they may not have seen its circularity. The inherent intelligence of the divines, their detection of circular proof in other arguments, and Owen's public criticism render this answer improbable. Indeed, Stillingfleet's attempt to bring in pagan, extrascriptural testimony shows some nervousness on his part that the proof cannot work on scriptural evidence alone. Second, the divines wished to establish rational evidences for scriptural truth, but not only internal evidence depending on reason in a narrow sense. They were conscious that if reason alone authenticates Scripture—if each discrete doctrine's contents are rationally measured—reason may end up being Scripture's worst enemy. For reason may begin to exclude from the *credenda* those articles it finds unfathomable, like the Trinity and Incarnation. The divines felt that although they could talk about these articles of faith rationally, a certain resistance to rationalization remains in the articles, indeed as their essence. The nature of their methodology continually alerted the divines never to pit reason against revelation. A rational proof from authority—an external rather than an internal argument—enabled them to overcome this impasse. Third, the divines labored to construct the elaborate argument from testimony because, once in place, it was very useful. At one stroke, given the fact of God's confirmation of the authors by miracles, all the contents of Scripture—doctrine, history, and prophecy—could be "rationally" accounted true.

In their discussions of the rational content of doctrines in Scripture, the divines had one overriding guideline: that once "divine revelation" is proved—that there is a God who has revealed himself, through the human authors, in Scripture—it is churlish to examine every doctrine in an impartial way. Tillotson writes: "Every man who believes the Holy Scriptures to be a truly Divine Revelation, does implicitly believe a great part of the prophetical books of Scripture, and several obscure expressions in those books, though he does not particularly understand the meaning of all the predictions and expressions contained in them."[26] Anglican apologetics were interested primarily in proving the fundamentals of Christianity; although divines frequently discussed the reasonableness of this or that particular doctrine, they refused to consider themselves bound to cover the whole field.

Barrow was especially strong on this point. Drawing on his background in mathematics, he insisted that theological methodology, in certain aspects, does not differ from that of science, even if the first principles of each rest on different types of evidence:

The principles of any science being either demonstrated out of some higher science, or evidenced by fit examples and experiments to common sense, and being thence granted and received 'tis afterward unlawfull and absurd to refuse the conclusions collected from them; so it have been proved that our principles are true; (for instance, that God is perfectly veracious, and that the Christian Religion hath his authority or attestation to it) 'twill then be part of absurd levity and inconsistency then to question any particular proposition evidently contained therein.

An infidel is free to examine impartially, he concludes, but it is "vain and inconstant" for a Christian to do so. In fact, he thereby "renounces the whole, and subverts the foundation of his faith; at least ceases thereby to be a steady Christian."[27]

Thus, though a Christian has rational grounds for being so—the great theme of much of the divines' writing—he does not treat each and every doctrine of his faith as though it were a still-to-be-proven first principle. The authority of Scripture, which holds Christian doctrine, may be externally proved; the general concept of divine revelation may also be shown to be reasonable. These generic proofs should suffice for rational assent to individual doctrines. The great cornerstone of this structure of rational proof is the argument from authority. Once in place, its strength may be supposed in every article of scriptural faith. That its strength may be deceptive, that it may hide a flaw, is a possibility the divines either did not or would not entertain.

III

Two other proofs, one internal, one external, that were often used in the later seventeenth century to discuss the truth of Scripture should be noticed. The first concerns prophecy, that is, the fulfillment by Jesus of the prophecies of the Old Testament about a Messiah who is to come. "The proof of the completion of Prophecies by Chronology," writes George Bright, "is a matter of great importance, to assure us that there hath been such a thing as Revelation in the World, by one of the greatest Miracles, the prediction of contingent futurities."[28] Most major divines were perfunctory in their discussion of prophecies; Gilbert Burnet, bishop of Salisbury, and Tillotson offered particularly concise summaries of allegedly Messianic passages from Moses and the prophets.[29] New Testament fulfillment of prophecies does not argue precisely to the truth of Scripture as such; Tillotson discussed the meaning of the prophecies under the heading of the means Jesus used to convince his contemporaries that he was the Messiah. Also, because the miracles of Jesus, some of which are foretold, authenticate his veracity, a close connection exists between the fulfilled prophecies and the truth of the New Testament. Few writers, however, joined Cudworth in his preference for the fulfilled prophecies, rather than miracles, as a proof of scriptural truth.[30] The divines apparently felt that a number of more fundamental matters must be discussed—natural religion, the possibility of revelation, the character of the authors—before the prophecies could be brought to bear in apologetics. The format of carefully structured works like *Origines Sacrae* and Ralph Barker's edition of Tillotson's *Sermons* makes this clear: discussion of prophecies therein is withheld until after more central matters are discussed.

A second minor proof, external in character, concerns the Holy Spirit. Notice of the Spirit's action in proving the truth of Scripture must remain a secondary proof because, as Sir Charles Wolseley writes, we know of the Spirit's existence in the Trinity only as a result of scriptural revelation.[31] The divines held, in traditional fashion, that the Spirit operates in the believer throughout the process of rational probation. Thus Chillingworth had assigned the Spirit the work of clearing up obscure places in Scripture: we must "wait his leasure" to make the plain sense clear.[32] In *Origines Sacrae* Stillingfleet summarizes the mainstream thought of the divines on the Spirit and Scripture: "When the Spirit *works* as to the *planting* of a truly *divine faith*, I do not think that it only *perswades* the *soul* of the *Truth* of a *Divine Testimony*, but withall represents the *Truths revealed* by that *Testimony*, with all that *excellency* and *suitableness* that there is in them, that by the most *agreeable*, yet *effectual influence* of the *Spirit* upon the *soul*, it cheerfully *embraceth* that *Truth* which is revealed, and *cordially* yields up its self in *obedience* to it."[33] Stillingfleet adds that "meer *rational evidence*" may satisfy the believer's mind, but only the Spirit causes effectual adherence to religion. Tillotson complements this emphasis: the Holy Spirit convinces us not so much of the truth of scriptural doctrine as of the fact that revelation is divine. The divines find a special connection between the work of the Spirit and the proof from testimony; the Spirit fills the gap, as it were, between the divines' claims for the argument and its suspected inadequacies. The Spirit seems to have less to do with rational proofs that are internal to Scripture; these seem more to be the work of readers themselves, without supernatural help. Both Stillingfleet and Tillotson stress that the Spirit lends an "abiding and effectual" character to faith.[34]

Robert South's contribution to the discussion of the role of the Spirit in helping faith is most interesting. The major divines stressed, against spokesmen for extrascriptural tradition and sectarian visionaries, that new revelation of the Spirit would not be forthcoming; of the four major divines, South writes most insistently on this point. He also has the most nuanced theory of how the Spirit works to convince us of scriptural revelation and, more surprisingly, of natural religion. South lists three functions of the Spirit in regard to faith. The second and third are routine: to give "notional Scriptural light" and "special convincing light," the former referring to a confirmation of ideas, the latter to that relish and taste for religion which Stillingfleet and Tillotson also assigned to the Spirit. In the first function, however, South associates the work of the Spirit with the work of reason itself. The "light of nature" and the "light of the Spirit" make up two aspects of the same phenomenon. Both refer to the "first dawning of the Spirit upon the soul, in those connate principles born with us into the world, and discovering, though very imperfectly, some general truths. As that there is a God, and that this God is to be worshipped, and the like." [35]

South mentions, in this context, that the Spirit was sent into the world at Jesus' death; he thus writes in the Johannine and Trinitarian tradition that is deeply scriptural, a tradition that is not usually associated, in the seventeenth century, with the formation of the truths of natural religion. South's perspective on these truths curiously contrasts with the theories of the fundamental notions, from Herbert of Cherbury onward, that are generally held to be epistemologically prior to their revelation in Scripture. Besides saying that these "general truths," which many think are natural, are the work of a supernatural spirit, South does not develop this point. Also, his brief discussion occurs in a sermon edited from his manuscripts after his death in 1716 and published in 1744. We do not know whether South would have developed this bridge between natural and supernatural religion had he finished editing his own manuscripts; the divines did not go out of the way elsewhere to develop such bridges. They were usually content to leave the affirmation of the truths of natural religion to reason alone, which needs no Spirit of God to operate.

So to base the truths of religion on reason rather than the Spirit implies a world of ordered, rational discourse, even perhaps of university education, royal visitations, and oaths to an established church. Acts of interpretation ascribed to the Spirit, on the contrary, are potentially revolutionary. John R. Knott distinguishes, for an earlier period, between those who sought "to confine the power for disruption implicit in Scripture" and those "who believed strongly in the kinetic power of the Word."[36] As Protestants, the divines believed in the kinetic power of Scripture; as figures of an establishment, indeed as its active creators, they were wary of the disruption Spirit-oriented interpretation had caused and might cause in the political arena. Nevertheless, the entire theological project of the divines should not be reduced to its political elements. In their attenuated theology of the Spirit the political impulse may figure strongly. In their larger orientation toward rational scriptural interpretation, they intended to be inclusive rather than exclusive, to put the ability to interpret Scripture on a broad basis, and to rise above the possibility of using Scripture for narrow political ends.

IV

In October 1694, John Locke wrote to a friend in Amsterdam, Philippus van Limborch, and asked for a full account of a reconversion to Christianity in which van Limborch had been instrumental. Early in December, van Limborch complied in a lengthy letter about a twenty-two-year-old woman, "fired with an incredible love of investigating the truth"; disenchanted with the arguments for Christianity of Reformed Dutch divines, she had turned to Judaism. Van Limborch dissuaded her from this step and carefully describes for Locke his method of argument, a method of which Locke obviously approved. Van Limborch first deemphasizes the arguments from prophecy and from scriptural doctrine such as the Trinity. Instead, he begins with the truth of the New Testament as a whole, concentrating particularly on the substantiating miracles of the Resurrection and the descent of the Holy Spirit on the Apostles at Pentecost. Avoiding the truth of the individual doctrines Scripture teaches, he concentrates on establishing the argument from testimony and miracles. Like Locke, van Limborch does not want to discuss disputed questions: "I asked her to pay no attention to the dogmas and theses of other men, of whatever sort they be, but only to the word of God."[37] Only after he establishes the truth of the New Testament does van Limborch turn, and then in some detail, to the prophecies of the Old. The length of van Limborch's account and Locke's interest in it suggest that they both considered the reconversion a model for all similar processes.

Van Limborch's treatment of scriptural truth is reminiscent in several ways of that of the Anglican divines of his day: the stress on the argument from miracles; the assumption of an absence of substantial corruption in the text of Scripture; and an insistence that his arguments do not possess mathematical certainty but are only "arguments to which nothing solid can be opposed, and which suffice for anyone devoted to the truth."[38] Yet as a whole, van Limborch's treatment markedly differs from that of the English divines. If only for the purpose of argument, he plays down the doctrinal content of Scripture in a way that is deeply counter to the divines' way of proceeding.

The divines carefully avoided the suggestion of a two-stage process in their apologetics for Scripture. For the purpose of analysis, I have separated the arguments from internal rationality of doctrine from those from external testimony; the divines rarely did so and generally envisioned a higher integration between the two arguments. In *Religio Laici* (1682), John Dryden offers a concise summary of this integration:

If on the Book it self we cast our view,
Concurrent Heathens prove the Story *True*:
The *Doctrine*, *Miracles*; which must convince,
For *Heav'n* in *Them* appeals to *humane Sense*:
And though they *prove* not, they *Confirm* the Cause,
When what is *Taught* agrees with *Natures Laws*.[39]

For Dryden, as for Stillingfleet, comparative history proves the historical narrative of the Old Testament true; the doctrine of Scripture is proved true by miracles, which also confirm God's authorship. "*Natures Laws*," or a stricter application of reason, act as a safeguard: scriptural doctrine never contradicts what God has also revealed, through nature, to reason. Dryden's plain style, confidently integrating these arguments in lucid syntax, makes a formal argument of its own. These arguments do not stand by themselves separately; they convince only when taken as a whole. The syntax asks the reader to move back and forth from argument to argument; these sometimes borrow each others' subjects and predicates inside one compound-complex sentence that visually and aurally creates the unity it asserts. Above all, Dryden's syntax avoids the hierarchy of arguments made by van Limborch and symbolizes the unity of the Anglican way of argument.

Sir Charles Wolseley, Dryden's chief source of argument in the poem, reinforces this Anglican view of the integration of scriptural proofs:

For as he [Jesus] frequently justifies his *Doctrine* from his *Miracles*, so he likewise often justifies his *Doctrine* to be in it self *Divine*, Corresponding to the Scriptures of the *Old Testament*, and in direct pursuance of what *Moses* and the *Prophets* had taught: And so makes the testimony of his Miracles unquestionable thereby; For such a Doctrine accompanied with such miraculous Evidence, must needs be from God, and can admit no Rational Opposition; And therefore, in discoursing this matter in hand, neither ought to be insisted on, neither the *Doctrine* nor the *Miracles*, *Distinctly* and *Separately* from the other, but *Both* urged in that excellent *Conjunction* in which they are handed down to us.[40]

In Wolseley's analysis, Jesus is reborn as an Anglican divine of the later seventeenth century, who carefully justifies the doctrine he preaches by both internal and external proofs. Like the divines, Jesus relies on miracles to prove doctrine; he also attempts to prove individual doctrines rational. The divines do this by reason, Jesus by their concordance with the teachings of the Old Testament. It is the "excellent *Conjunction*" of these two methodologies that Wolseley insistently calls to our attention.

Finally, Isaac Barrow also invokes the example of Jesus to show the inseparability of the proofs for scriptural truth. Of the apostles he writes:

Their faith was not merely founded upon authority, but relied partly upon the principles of reason, taking in the assistance and attestation of sense. They that beheld the sincerity and innocency of our Saviour's conversation; the extraordinary wisdom and majesty of his discourses; the excellent goodness and holiness of his doctrine; the incomparably great and glorious power discovered in his miraculous works (withal comparing the ancient prophecies concerning such a person to come with the characters and circumstances of his person), were by these considerations persuaded, not merely by his own testimony.[41]

In its easy movement from reason to sense, from internal to external evidences, and from history to universality, this passage shows how, for Barrow, the act of rational faith, for all its different bases of evidence, remains a smoothly psychological unity. In the world of real belief, Dryden, Wolseley, and Barrow assume that the various arguments for the truth of Scripture flow easily into one another.

In conclusion we may ask how "rational" this interdependent unity of arguments truly is. With firm confidence, the divines referred their readers and hearers back and forth, from internal to external, from prophecy to history. Yet the argument from internal rationality involves, as we have seen, only a few truths of Scripture concerning the doctrines of natural religion; the argument from testimony, involving miracles, assumes the truth of the very Scriptures it attempts to verify. Arguments from prophecy and history depend for their substantiation on that from testimony. The scriptural apologetics of the divines must rank very low in any hierarchy of rationalisms one might construct out of late seventeenth-century thought.

4

Scripture and Polity: Filmer, Locke, Butler, and Dryden

D̲uring the morning of June 26, 1650, Parliament decided a question that had been troubling its members for some weeks: who was to lead the proposed punitive invasion of Scotland? Sir Thomas Fairfax, the general of the army, was reluctant to do so; Parliament awarded him a yearly pension of £5,000, and he retired to his estates in Yorkshire. In his place, Parliament chose the obvious man, Oliver Cromwell, to become captain-general of the army. Cromwell was nervous about being chosen; he did not want to appear to be grasping for tyrannical power. During the afternoon of June 26 he decided to unburden himself to Edmund Ludlow, a thirty-three-year-old member from Wiltshire, a regicide like Cromwell, but one whom Cromwell suspected might question his motives. Ludlow later summarized the conversation:

He professed to desire nothing more than that the government of the nation might be settled in a free and equal Commonwealth, acknowledging that there was no other probable means to keep out the old family and government from returning upon us; declaring that he looked upon the design of the Lord in this day to be the freeing of His people from every burden, and that He was now accomplishing what was prophesied in the 110th Psalm; from the consideration of which he was often encouraged to attend the effecting of those ends, spending at least an hour in the exposition of that Psalm, adding to this, that it was his intention to contribute the utmost of his endeavours to make a thorow reformation of Clergy and Law.[1]

Although Ludlow later turned against Cromwell, and the subsequent *Memoirs* are not without bias, the very matter-of-factness of this recollection suggests its foundation in history.

Indeed the tone clashes with the recollection's extraordinary content. Allegorical readings of Scripture that applied the Old Testament to contemporary political change were common in the later seventeenth century; Charles II and James II routinely subsidized poets who depicted them in biblical terms. What is extraordinary about Ludlow's account is the seriousness and length of Cromwell's exegesis and also the prominent part the exegete himself plays in fulfilling the prophecies involved.

In the Geneva translation, Psalm 110 reads:

[1] The Lord said unto my Lord, sit thou at my right hand, until I make thine enemies thy footstoole.

[2] The Lord shall send the rod of thy power out of Sion: bee thou ruler in the midst of thine enemies.

[3] Thy people *shall come* willingly at the time of *assembling* thine armie in holy beauty: the youth of thy wombe *shall be* as the morning dew.

[4] The Lord sware, and will not repent, Thou art a Priest forever after the order of Melchi-zedek.

[5] The Lord *that is* at thy right hand, shall wound kings in the day of his wrath.

[6] He shall be judge among the heathen: hee shall fill *all* with dead bodies, *and* smite the head over great countries.

[7] He shall drinke out of the brooke in the way, therefore shall hee lift up *his* head.

In a marginal note to verse 1, the editors of the Geneva translation write that, because Jesus quotes this Psalm in the New Testament (Matthew 22:44), the Psalm "cannot properly be applied to David."[2] That is, the literal sense of the passage, that which tells about the history of the author, must in this case give way to its allegorical meaning, that which refers to the Messiah who is to come. Although the Geneva editors did not concern themselves with postscriptural fulfillments of the Psalm, their dismissal of the literal sense allowed Cromwell his extraordinary exegetical flight.

Granted the allegorical option, much in Psalm 110 could be seen to predict events in England and in Cromwell's life before and during the summer of 1650. He had overcome his enemies within and without his own side (verses 1, 2); he would shortly leave England at the head of an army (verses 2, 3); the kings and princes of England and Ireland had been dealt with, occasionally, as in Ireland, in the midst of great slaughter (verses 5, 6); after escaping from Carisbrooke Castle in 1647, Charles I was defeated and executed in 1649 (verse 7). The final "head" may be Cromwell's own, destined to wear a literal or metaphorical crown; or it may be Charles I's, whose bloody head, held aloft by the executioner, became the cornerstone, as Andrew Marvell writes in "An Horatian Ode," of republican England. If in fact Cromwell's exegesis of the prophecy of Psalm 110 lasted for the hour Ludlow says it did, Cromwell entered into specific fulfillments of its verses in far more detailed and fanciful ways than those offered here.

Only the apparent intensity and self-involvement of Cromwell's exegesis distance it from many attempts, even after 1660, to understand contemporary English polity as in some way reflected in scriptural texts. Scripture was used to affirm or deny specific forms of polity after 1660 in several complex ways; I hope in this chapter to survey and order a few basic applications of Scripture to polity made in the period. In a manner similar to Cromwell's exegesis, there were many attempts, particularly at the time of the Restoration and of Charles's coronation a year later, to picture the restored king as a new Noah, Moses, and David. This use of Scripture implies but does not always explicitly enunciate the absoluteness of the king's power, as one elected by God to lead the new chosen people, England. Other writers, including the major divines, whose loyalty to Charles is undoubted, avoided specific scriptural analogies and used Scripture as a manual for the relations that should exist between governor and governed. One group of political thinkers held that the

Bible contains explicit norms for a polity of patriarchal government; still another, on whose fringes radical thought existed, completely denied the legitimacy of such a use of Scripture.

From a survey of the uses of Scripture to establish or disestablish a specific polity after 1660, we gain two insights. First, so great was the weight of Scripture in the period that it was seemingly impossible to theorize upon the nature of the state or the monarchy without casting their origins, existence, and maintenance in scriptural terms. This approach might be expected of those advocating the divine election of the king, but continued reference to Scripture also occurs in the writings of those exploring theories of the social contract. Second, it is difficult to associate in this period particular methods of reading Scripture with particular theories of the state. This is especially true of writers with a strong monarchical bent. Some are as explicit in their connections of Old Testament historical narrative with contemporary events as Cromwell was in his. Perhaps perceiving that such allegorizing is a double-edged tool and can be used to support even regicide, others warned against allegorical readings, especially of Davidic materials, at the same time as they used other parts of Scripture to uphold a near-absolute monarchy. A third group of writers who, in following John Locke, promoted the social contract, were more consistent: they avoided allegorical readings but used literal and tropological readings of Scripture to buttress their theory. Indeed, arguments over the meanings of a number of texts of Scripture form the principal battleground between new and old theories of polity.

One common seventeenth-century form of relating Scripture to secular polity involved "typology." Cromwell's attempts to picture himself as the new David, sent by God to purify and aggrandize the kingdom, represent the typological mentality at its starkest. Such a reading of the Psalms presupposes a broad providential scheme involving not only God's general providence over his creation but also his "special providence" in regard to certain nations. This special providence elects certain nations as its own, then sends that nation leaders to promote its welfare. Point-by-point correspondences are found in the different historical appearances, in Scripture and in the contemporary scene, of such providential leaders. Thus both David and Cromwell crush kings in their rise to power; both Moses and Charles II leave a foreign land, crossing through a sea, to lead their peoples to their destinies.[3] Recent scholarship on political typology after 1660 has made us aware—if the poems of Dryden are adequate cultural indexes—that such a typology was on the wane in the period or at least was undergoing qualitative change.[4] It was certainly easier to call Charles II a new Moses in 1660 and 1661 than to apply a similar analogy to his brother-successor in the 1680s. Political typology is living and changing, and it maintained itself as a form of political discourse well into the eighteenth century; but for a number of reasons, including the general unpopularity of James II and demythologizing advances in political philosophy, typology became increasingly hollow after the country's initial burst of enthusiasm in 1660.

When Cromwell accomplished his exegesis of Psalm 110 in 1650, we presume that he was serious; such self-analysis in scriptural terms is part of the accepted meaning of the term "Puritan." When a prose or verse writer after 1660 compared England to Israel and Charles II to one of Israel's leaders, it is often very difficult to estimate the seriousness of the analogy. When Bishop George Morley, the preacher at Charles's coronation on April 23, 1661, compared the king's rebuilding of his realm with David's restoration of the walls of Sion, he may have intended to read and enunciate a recurrent divine plan. But when Edmund Waller compared the king's early-1660s improvements in St. James's Park to the creation of Eden, and the king himself to Orpheus, the patriarchs of Genesis, Augustus, Hercules, and Jesus Christ, we may smile.[5] Because Waller and many other poets were royalists, and because they characterized the period following the Restoration as an era of wit, it is sometimes too easy to assume that such writers were not serious. Yet wit itself, in the seventeenth century, not only created comedy but was also a faculty for discovering analogies between various levels of reality, including historical reality.

Many in England around the time of the Restoration believed that God specially intervened in European history in the safe and peaceful return of Charles II, in a way that could best be understood as an analogy of what God accomplished in Israel's history. Edward Hyde, earl of Clarendon, generally excluded typological interpretation and supernatural causality from his histories; yet when attempting to explain the sudden change in the English political climate in 1659 and 1660, Hyde joined many less sophisticated commentators in resort to typology. He could attribute the king's return only to "such a prodigious act of Providence as he hath scarce vouchsafed to any nation, since he led his own chosen people through the Red Sea."[6] At least for some time after the Restoration, then, serious thinkers found straightforward political typology a convenient and even inevitable method to discuss recent political changes. Use of the term "typology" to characterize descriptions of political events in this time does not mean only "poetic imagery," as if the connection between the king and prophets and patriarchs existed only in poets' or historians' minds. The possibility must be entertained that the correspondence between type and antitype was truly believed to exist objectively, that is, in the context of some specially providential scheme of divine and salvific activity in England.

II

Though written in the late 1640s, Sir Robert Filmer's treatise *Patriarcha* had no printed version until 1680, and then an incomplete one. Edmund Bohun published a more complete second edition in 1685; it was not until 1949 that Peter Laslett edited and published a definitive text, based on the discovery of an autograph copy.[7] In discussing Filmer's use of Scripture to establish the ultra-royalist theory of *Patriarcha*, the date of its composition is important. Filmer shows no evidence of being aware of ongoing movements in Anglican scriptural interpretation, especially their increasing insistence on the historical and literal sense. These movements arose during his lifetime (1588–1653) but reached their apogee only after 1660.

Similar chronological reasons also explain Filmer's lack of awareness of the newer, critical methods of reading Scripture proposed by Hobbes in 1650 and Spinoza in 1670. It has often been said that the value of *Patriarcha* lies not so much in its own political theory as in the pressure it put on its adversaries to refine alternate theories of polity. The same is true about the use of Scripture in *Patriarcha*: Filmer's mode of interpreting Scripture is naive, but his methods helped others to define a proper way of discussing polity in scriptural terms.

"Sir Robert Filmer's prime assumption," writes Laslett, "was that the Bible was the true, unique and complete revelation of God's will on all things."[8] In scriptural revelation Filmer finds the directions for the political welfare of mankind, which, in the seventeenth century, was not conceptually distinct from its spiritual welfare. Especially in its account of human origins, in Genesis, Scripture teaches not only theological but political truth. By creating one man first, God intended that all political power and all property should accrue to him. The later creation and generation of woman and children, precisely because they are subsequent to the creation of Adam, imply that they are, in God's plan, subordinate to him. At Adam's death, his patriarchal dominion is transferred to his surviving firstborn male, in a repetition of God's original donation. The creation of Adam is thus not only a scriptural "fact" for Filmer; it is also a source of eternal value. Adam's prime role as patriarch and owner of the earth functions as a normative account of how political power must always occur. All men and women born into the world are born as Eve and her children were: as subjects radically oriented in obedience to the patriarch or his legitimate descendant. We should not get bogged down in trying to determine who, in the seventeenth century, was thought to be the legitimate descendant of Adam, inheriting his patriarchal power, for Filmer, though he clearly has his eye on Charles I, does not. Although *Patriarcha* is a mixed bag of royalist pleading and philosophical analysis, we may give Filmer the benefit of the doubt: the tract is at least as interested in asserting that political mankind is born into patriarchy as it is in resolving the chaos at the end of Charles I's reign.

Filmer bases his argument for the patriarchal nature of human society on commonplace royalist readings of the Old Testament.[9] We may ask what rules for scriptural interpretation such readings, as least in *Patriarcha*, involve. First, Filmer often argues not so much from the literal sense of Scripture as from its silence. On the question of the passing down of the "donation" to Adam to future generations, for example, Filmer argues not from the text but from the improbability of a different power from that Adam was given: "It is not probable that the private dominion which God gave to Adam, and, by his donation, assignation or cession to his children, was abrogated, and a community of all things instituted between Noah and his sons!"[10] That is, in the absence of a direct scriptural account, we may assume that an abrogation of patriarchy did not take place between Adam and Noah's time—and, indeed, even up to the seventeenth century. Examples of such an argument could easily be multiplied. Laslett notes that Filmer mentally dwelled on and drew inferences from a period about which Scripture is relatively silent, that period when Adam lived alone.[11] Such meditation on the silent interstices of the scriptural account enabled Filmer more confidently to assert Adam's supremacy.

Second, it is common to talk of Filmer's "literal" or "slavishly literal" reading of Genesis.[12] Filmer's arguments from probability and silence, however, imply that he was undertaking something more than a literal reading. Even more important in this regard is Filmer's repeated practice of reading key texts such as the granting of dominion to Adam (Genesis 1:28) and to Cain (Genesis 4:7) not only literally but in a fashion that might be called, for want of a more exact term, allegorically. That is, Filmer holds that such texts contain within them not only a literal account of how things came to be but also a normative account of how things must always be; the founding of a primitive state contains in itself the objective foundation for all states. I do not mean that Filmer simply uses Scripture to establish the rules for the behavior of children to parents and subjects to monarchs; even John Locke, Filmer's most noted adversary, used Scripture in this moral or tropological way. Filmer also understands the donation to Adam as a process objectively repeated in frequent divine interventions in the Old Testament. The donation to Adam—in this sense, a type—sets up an objective pattern God vouchsafes to repeat, in numerous antitypes, throughout history.

If we assume that the readership of *Patriarcha*, in its manuscript and printed versions, was large and included royalist poets, a curious richness accrues to their biblical imagery. For example, Dryden's "To His Sacred Majesty, A Panegyrick on His Coronation" (1661) begins with an involved comparison of Charles landing in England and Noah on Mount Ararat.[13] On one level, this comparison of Charles to Noah implies simple, rhetorical amplification; Dryden aggrandizes the antitype by situating him in reference to the Old Testament. On another level, rhetoric becomes theology: the king, if we take the typology seriously, has become another instance of God's election of leaders to guide his people in perilous times. In the context of *Patriarcha*—if we assume Dryden knew of a manuscript version—the theological rhetoric becomes political discourse as well. By calling Charles Noah, the poem may also suggest a transferral to him of Noah's patriarchal power. In the complexity of the typological image, Charles also becomes the literal and valid inheritor of the donation of power and property made, in Filmer's analysis, to the patriarchs.

To disentangle metaphor and to insist that the allegorical be challenged by the literal is always tedious business. Perhaps this is why, even in our own day, interpreters of Locke have found his *Essay Concerning False Principles*, the first of his *Two Treatises of Government* (1690), tedious. Locke takes Filmer seriously when, if we stress Filmer's connections with the political verse of the Restoration, we may prefer to categorize his work, like the verse, as playful anachronism. Nevertheless, we must be careful to distinguish Locke's precise point of view in the first treatise, which deals entirely with a refutation of Filmer. Neither here nor in *An Essay Concerning the True Original, Extent, and End of Civil Government*, the second treatise, does Locke argue that Scripture cannot offer rules or advice to seventeenth-century political philosophy. His premises on the relation of Scripture and polity are twofold. First, if Scripture addresses polity, it must be in its literal or moral senses; polity is too important a subject to become lost in a maze of allegorical readings. Second, even after we have established what Scripture literally has to say about the origin and conduct of government, we must go beyond Scripture to an analysis of human nature. Scripture does not contain all truth about all things. Rather, reason and scriptural revelation must be mined together to build up a true theory of government.

Again and again in *An Essay Concerning False Principles*, Locke appeals to the literal sense of Scripture to demonstrate the falsity of a patriarchal theory of government. The texts Filmer used to support such a theory, Locke argues, cannot be used, in their literal sense, for that purpose. Of the key Filmerite text concerning the Adamic donation, Locke writes:

'Tis nothing but the giving to Man, the whole Species of Man, as the chief inhabitant, who is the Image of his Maker, the Dominion over the other Creatures. This lies so obvious in the plain words, that any one but our *A*. [Author: Filmer] would have thought it necessary to have shewn, how these words that seem'd to say the quite contrary, gave *Adam Monar-*

chical Absolute Power over other Men, or the *Sole Property* in all the Creatures, and methinks in a business of this moment, and that whereon he builds all that follows, he should have done something more than barely cite words which apparently make against him.[14]

Locke argues that Filmer's interpretation of the blessing of Noah is also biased against "the plain express words of the Scripture," "the plain construction of the words," "the obvious meaning of the place," and "the direct and plain meaning of the Words." Of Filmer's interpretation of the donation to Cain as a proof for patriarchy, Locke writes: "It is too much to build a Doctrine of so mighty consequence upon so doubtful and obscure a place of Scripture, which may be well, nay better, understood in a quite different Sense, and so can be but an ill Proof, being as doubtful as the thing to be proved by it, especially when there is nothing else in Scripture or Reason to be found, that favours or supports it."[15] In the place of Filmer's particularist, prejudiced readings of Genesis texts, Locke insists on a rational reading of Scripture that accords with the teaching of the whole of Scripture, and that is, above all, literal.

The exact attitude of Locke toward Scripture as a basis for polity has not always been perceived correctly. Locke does not say that the rules for polity are found nowhere in Scripture. He does say that, if they are in Scripture, they must be found in the literal, plain sense, and that the rules Filmer sets out are clearly not so. A modern reader may think Locke to be avoiding the issue here. He denies that one form of polity is literally taught in Scripture in the first treatise; in the second treatise he bases a contractual polity mainly though not entirely on rational analysis of human nature. Is it not implied that Scripture says nothing to the formation of the modern state? The whole of Locke's work does not justify such a conclusion. Like many Anglicans of the late seventeenth century, Locke believed in the mutuality of the formulations of reason in its analysis of human nature and of what Scripture teaches.

The second treatise amply illustrates such mutuality. The use of Scripture in the second treatise is complex, as it is in many of the theological tracts and sermons of the period. Locke's analysis of two cardinal problems—the state of nature and the right to property—shows his easy movement from reason to Scripture as sources for a modern theory of polity. Chapter 2 of *An Essay Concerning the True Original, Extent, and End of Civil Government*, justly prized for its clarity and common sense, though several times alluding to such scriptural doctrines as creationism and the *lex talionis*, depends for its force not on Scripture but on a rational analysis of human nature and the natural freedom given to human beings as their birthright. Locke quotes Richard Hooker's *Laws of Ecclesiastical Polity* to show that the natural equality of humanity is "evident in itself, and beyond all question";[16] reason can arrive at no other conclusion but that we are born not in subordination one to another, at least in a political sense, but, until we contract ourselves into society, in perfect freedom. Locke neither needs nor uses Scripture to prove such a fundamental point, although certain doctrines ancillary to it, such as the denial of a right of self-destruction, are obviously informed by scriptural morality. At this point in the second treatise, Locke relies heavily on the evidence of reason and of authority (e.g., Hooker); scriptural evidence is not available for the doctrine of natural right and only implicitly brought to bear for its corollaries.

At the start of chapter 5 of the second treatise, on property, Locke says that both "natural *Reason*" and scriptural "*Revelation*" testify that "'tis very clear, that God, as King *David* says, *Psal.* CXV.XVI. *has given the Earth to the Children of Men*, given it to Mankind in common."[17] How, then, does private property arise? Both reason and Scripture answer this question:

God, when He gave the World in common to all Mankind, commanded Man also to labour, and the penury of his condition required it of him. God and his Reason commanded him to subdue the Earth, i.e. improve it for the benefit of Life, and therein lay out something upon it that was his own, his labour. He that in Obedience to this Command of God, subdued, filled, and sowed any part of it, thereby annexed to it something that was his *Property*, which another had no Title to, nor could without injury take from him.[18]

Thus Locke establishes the history of and right to private property on the evidence of both scriptural injunction and a rational analysis of the human condition. The arguments easily fold into one another, as might be expected in the writings of a late seventeenth-century critical believer, as Locke was. Though most of the second treatise does not argue its political philosophy on the evidence of Scripture, occasional use of scriptural precedent and injunction show Locke's easy assumption of the mutuality of rational analysis and scriptural authority. The second treatise is not, like the first, a treatise on scriptural interpretation; although drawing mainly from the evidence of reason, it exhibits no nervousness that any of its arguments say anything against those parts of Scripture whose literal or moral sense may be plainly construed to address polity.

Reading the *Two Treatises* in the context of the Anglican method of interpreting Scripture in Locke's time, one is struck by the profound analogies between the evidentiary methodology of Locke and that of the divines. These analogies exist even though the entities—Locke's political theory and the divines' theology—are somewhat different. Both Locke and the divines considered only the literal and moral senses of Scripture as a sure foundation for beliefs binding on all Christians. Neither a necessary creed nor form of polity can rest on an easily disputable and partisan allegorical sense. Also, as in the divines' discussion of first principles, Locke's political philosophy appeals to a nonscriptural, rational given. In theology, this given is the existence of God; in politics, it is the human birthright of freedom and equality. Such an appeal presupposes a concordance between reason and Scripture; God, who speaks both in reason and Scripture, has arranged that they supplement each other. Finally, because Locke, in the *Two Treatises*, deals not with eternal salvation but with mankind's temporal condition, he moves more freely away from Scripture in articulating this condition. Easy correspondence with Scripture, however, is maintained. At times Locke uses scriptural evidence merely as historical precedent; at times the precedent legitimates problematic current politics. Thus, because God blessed Hezekiah's attempts to overthrow Assyrian control of Judah, rebellion is not always an offense against him.[19] In his negative critique of Filmer's partisan scriptural interpretation and his lesser, positive use of scriptural evidence in the second treatise, Locke works from the same principles of scriptural interpretation as do the divines.

A few minor figures writing to support Filmer or Locke provide interesting glosses on their methods of scriptural interpretation. In his long preface to the second edition, in 1685, of *Patriarcha*, Edmund Bohun, Filmer's editor, maintains the Filmerite position that patriarchy is based on Scripture. Writing more than thirty years after *Patriarcha* had been written, and aware of interpretational problems raised against it, Bohun is somewhat more studied than Filmer had been in arguing out and explaining his own logic and probabilistic reasoning. Indeed, Bohun's common sense occasionally undermines the simplicity of Filmer's arguments. Bohun notes the objection that if God gave all power and all property to Adam and then to Cain, why does he not continue to do so? Should not the precedent of Scripture be rigorously followed, if Scripture is forever the norm? Bohun answers: "It is utterly impossible that one Man should govern the whole World, and therefore that could never be the intention of God when he gave *Cain* a power over *Abel*." [20] Once one admits the evidence of the rationally "impossible," a category informed by an analysis of contemporary society, it can be turned in a number of ways. Cannot patriarchy, in seventeenth-century England, also be understood as a rational impossibility? Once the rigor of Filmer's allegorical interpretation of any part of Scripture is undermined, a new set of interpretive principles is needed to determine why other parts of Scripture must still be accorded Filmerite interpretation.

On the Lockean side, scriptural interpretation becomes less finely nuanced, and we see a variety of ways in which Locke's alternate use of Scripture and reason may be transformed into something less complex. Like Locke, Algernon Sidney argued with Filmer's interpretation of Scripture but did not deny Scripture's usefulness in formulating a polity. Of the alleged necessity to repeat the patriarchal political system, in an essay published long after his execution for attempted regicide in 1683, Sidney writes:

It is hard to imagine, that God, who hath left all things to our choice, that are not evil in themselves, should tie us up in this; and utterly incredible that he should impose upon us a necessity of following his will, without declaring it to us. Instead of constituting a government over his people, consisting of many parts, which we take to be a model fit to be imitated by others, he might have declared in a word, that the eldest man of the eldest line should be king; and that his will ought to be their law. This had been more suitable to the goodness and mercy of God, than to leave us in a dark labyrinth, full of precipices; or rather, to make the government given to his own people, a false light to lead us to destruction.[21]

The argument is complicated. If we are left to ourselves to devise a polity, and God gives us the freedom to do so, we would establish one "of many parts," a system of checks and balances, in which the monarchy and other social classes, at least the aristocracy and landowners, would be adequately represented. Filmer, however, states that Scripture teaches patriarchy, an absolutism that does not allow for broad sharing of power. Sidney presents this problem in a way that the evidence of reason and Scripture might be thought at odds, a presentation that Locke avoids. Sidney resolves the problem, however, as Locke does: Filmer does not in fact present the teaching of the literal sense of Scripture; "the goodness and mercy of God" would allow scriptural teaching about polity to be communicated only as clear and distinct injunctions, and certainly not in the "dark labyrinth" of Filmerite interpretation. The problem of opposition between reason and Scripture is thus seen to be a false one. Sidney also occasionally uses Scripture as a positive source of polity: the Judaic political system, for example, was aristocratic, not monarchical, and Scripture says that safeguards should be placed on kings.[22] Nevertheless, in its nuances if not in its conclusion, Sidney's argument envisions a situation that might force political thinkers to choose between reason and Scripture.

James Tyrell and Thomas Rymer, two other opponents of patriarchalism in the early 1680s, moved further from the Lockean synthesis. Tyrell, who corresponded with Locke, also argued that Filmer had not grasped the literal sense of the words of Genesis.[23] As a whole, however, Tyrell's methodology avoids use of positive evidence from Scripture, "the Scripture not being written," as he says, "to teach us Politicks, but to declare God's Will."[24] A step in principle as well as methodology toward a divorce between reason and Scripture as evidences for polity was taken by Rymer, a literary critic, antiquarian, and eventually historiographer royal, in his *A General Draught and Prospect of Government in Europe, and Civil Policy, Shewing the Antiquity, Power, and Decay of Parliaments* (1681). This short work may be considered as a republican warhorse, taken out of its

stable when the cause of a Whig parliament was threatened: first published during the exclusion crisis, a second edition came out in 1704 and a
third in 1714. Whig politicians found Rymer's argument, though somewhat crabbed in its presentation, a useful ally; it is that a parliamentary
system is the natural condition of European government.

Rymer is very clear on the place of Scripture in formulating political
theory:

Then for the Holy Scripture; the design of it is no more to teach us Politicks than to make us Philosophers . . . where ever Christ is Preached the
Soul-saving Doctrine in no wise operates upon the policy or civil Consti-
tutions; but leaves those affairs to be influenc'd by the ordinary prudence
and discretion. . . .

All power is from God, and we are subject to the higher powers; this
all consent to; this is a Doctrine alike true in *Holland*, as in *France*, at *Ven-
ice*, as at *Constantinople*.

But where this high power and Sovereignty rests, in Whom 'tis lodged,
this is a point not so obvious: Nor can the S. S. or the holy Fathers any-
way help us in the discovery.[25]

Rymer blatantly voids all contemporary Davidic reference by distinguishing between the Psalms and the political theory of David, the shepherd-
king: "A shepherd, not withstanding the Oracles he delivered, continued
the same in other circumstances, as if he had never been inspir'd."[26]

The difference between Locke and Rymer presents, in a microcosm,
many of the difficulties one faces in trying to understand the interplay of
reason and Scripture in both the theology and politics of the later seventeenth century. Locke and Rymer both argue that a contractual or representative government is the natural state of mankind in Europe. Yet the
matrix of Locke's argument from reason and Scripture is much older and
more traditional, a methodology echoed in the work of the divines of his
day, who presumed a unity in the knowledge one may achieve from both
sources. Rymer's position resembles Spinoza's: we do not go to Scripture
to learn philosophy, for it refuses "to make us Philosophers." Unlike
Locke, Rymer also avoids the usual moral readings of Scripture as a manual of the relations between government and governed. We are forced to

discriminate, then, between the rational analyses of Locke and Rymer, concerning polity, as we must between, for example, Barrow and Spinoza on the meaning of faith and belief. One analysis exists—even as it is enunciating new formulas and creeds—firmly in a tradition; the other is a rationalism, drawing its strength from a heritage that was being newly articulated in the dawn of Enlightenment thought.

III

Less than three years before the day in 1650 when Cromwell took Ludlow aside to explicate the typology of Psalm 110, one of Cromwell's most illustrious opponents, to console himself in exile, embarked upon a systematic explication of the entire 150 Psalms. As Cromwell turned to the Psalms in triumph, Edward Hyde, future earl of Clarendon, turned to them for solace in defeat. The history of the composition of Hyde's *Contemplations and Reflections upon the Psalms of David, Applying Those Devotions to the Troubles of the Times* reflects the alternating sun and shadows of his career. He wrote his commentary on the first seventy Psalms in the late 1640s, while in exile on Jersey; again in exile, he finished the commentary at Montpellier in the late 1660s.

In his preface of 1671, Hyde distinguishes three frames of reference through which the Psalms usually have been interpreted. The first involves typological interpretation, which he finds full of difficulty. Some believe, he writes, "almost every one of the *Psalms* to contain some Prophecy of our Saviour"; but such an interpretation raises many textual difficulties, causes hyperbolical interpretation, and resorts to insistence on metaphorical language. Second, the interpreter may concentrate on the "easy Places" in the Psalms, "which by being easy, are most useful and applicable to the several Conditions of our Life, which we may fall into, whether we are in Joy or Sorrow, in any Perplexity or Distress, and under any of God's dispensations." Thus Hyde's own "Perplexity or Distress" in the late 1640s and 1660s led him to the Davidic Psalms of exile— not to image himself as a new David but to receive comfort from the pious writings of a fellow exile.

Third, we rightly interpret the Psalms literally, that is, in the historical context of David's life. Hyde considers this interpretation distinctly modern and Anglican, as the first is archaic and the second of universal application: "Many of our modern or later Divines, to be compared for their great Learning and sound Knowledge to any who have been before them, are of Opinion, that there are not many Psalms which may not be very naturally and literally applied to those very Occasions, and the particular State that David was then in, when he poured out those Devotions, though all do not agree upon the Subject, and the Occasion." [27]

Hyde's evaluation of methods for reading the Psalms—which roughly correspond to allegorical, moral, and literal readings—accords with that of the major divines after 1660. Though much typology remained in the period's verse and sermons, the major divines generally avoided it. They usually reserved typological interpretation for its primary function: because Jesus fulfilled the Old Testament prophecies concerning the Messiah, he rightly lays claim to that role. The divines generally eschewed the extension of such typology from the scriptural to the political context; the detailed political exegesis of Scripture, as practiced by Cromwell in June 1650 and also by many royalists after 1660, was completely alien to the practice of the major divines. Such reticence did not prevent the divines from applying the moral sense of Scripture to the highs and lows of human existence, including political existence. As in Hyde's case, personal and communal joys and sorrows may have political causes; but it is the universal aspects of even political experience that Scripture illuminates. Thus Hyde interprets Psalm 110, in the course of his commentary, as a reminder to Israel of all that God has done for it, and to contemporary readers of the even greater gift of the gospel, which they inexcusably forget. [28]

That a historical human being, King David, recorded his experience in enduring literary form supports this second use of Scripture as a moral address to universal human problems. In their sermons, the divines, like Hyde, habitually exploited both his second and third frames of reference. It is common for many sermons to locate a Davidic text historically before setting out, at greater length, moral application. As Archbishop William Sancroft writes in such a sermon in 1678, "David's History is the proper Key to *David's* Psalter; and so the Books of *Samuel*, the *Kings*, and *Chronicles*, the best, and most authentick Commentary upon the

Psalms."[29] Thus the standard post-1660 method of interpreting the Psalms—and, indeed, all of Scripture—requires serious effort at recovering the literal sense, on which moral lessons may be based, and a studied avoidance of typological interpretation.

We may ask whether such an avoidance of typology was subversive, in that it clearly disagreed with the methods of many court poets, including John Dryden, whom Charles and James subsidized. Yet subversion cannot explain the practice of Hyde, whose loyalty was clear; nor did the major divines fail to honor the Stuart prerogative in ways other than typology. Nor can we say that typology was generally considered tainted by its use by Puritans; royalist indulgence in typology is simply too evident after 1660. It is more likely that the major divines simply felt that politically typological interpretation of Scripture, once admitted, tended to excess. This would be true both historically, as it had been used in the Interregnum, and also philosophically, for the divines felt that the abandonment of literal interpretation in any area would eventually lead to a chaos of theological evidences. As Tillotson writes of those who sought to parallel English misfortune with previous occasions of divine punishment: "Everything hath two handles; and good wit and strong imagination may find some thing in every Judgement, whereby he may with some appearance of Reason turn the cause of the Judgement upon his Adversary. Fancy is an endless thing, and if we will go this way to work, then he that hath the best Wit, is like to be the best interpreter of God's Judgements."[30] The context is not exclusively scriptural, but Tillotson's wariness of excess is always evident in his and his fellow divines' application of scriptural history to contemporary affairs.

Tillotson also underscores the major problems involved in such a process. Once the anchor of the literal sense is lost, by what authority do we discriminate valid from invalid, or legitimate from seditious typologies? Fancy is endless, and stability in interpretation can be achieved only by an authority outside the text—either public or private subsidy of typological literature or, negatively, censorship. An appeal to external authority to solve interpretive difficulties, for it denigrated the Protestant principle of *sola Scriptura* and smacked of Hobbism or Rome, was always suspect to the divines. "Although 'providential' theories of history did not lose their vogue," writes Christopher Hill of the period after 1660, "the fact that partisans of both sides in the civil war used such arguments weakened their effectiveness (as against the days when there still had been a consensus among the literate—or when censorship made it appear that there was a consensus)."[31] If political typology can be used by both sides in a war as self-justification, then it follows that the meaning of Scripture is ambiguous in such an important matter as civil rebellion; the divines' insistence that Scripture in essentials is plain and clear led them to denigrate political, typological readings as the creation of ingenious readers rather than of inspired authors.

Of the major divines, only Robert South consistently preached about political reality; Barrow, Stillingfleet, and Tillotson addressed political contexts only when they could not avoid it—for example, when they were asked to preach on days of national commemoration such as January 30 (the regicide) or November 5 (the Gunpowder Plot), or in times of national crisis, such as the Popish Plot. Irène Simon has ably cataloged the political thinking of the major divines in the only way such a catalog can be accomplished, preacher by preacher, sermon by sermon, in their exact contexts. She concludes:

In their statements on the relation between spiritual and temporal powers divines took care not to suggest submission of the Church to the State. . . . What they envisaged, in fact, was an amicable collaboration between the two powers, as had been envisaged in the Elizabethan Settlement. By not pressing a definite theory the Church ensured a measure of flexibility in its relation with the State. . . . The Anglican clergy did not resist the notion that civil authority derives from the people; most of them did sanction the theory of Divine Right; all of them taught passive obedience.[32]

It is not surprising that such a fluid, inconsistent set of beliefs was able to accommodate oath-taking to William of Orange in 1688–89.[33]

Before and after 1688, the political sermons of the divines tended to center on a number of texts which enjoin obedience to the monarchy and prayers for it (for example, Romans 13:2, 1 Timothy 2:2, Psalm 144:10, 1 Samuel 26:9). Thus the divines made a positive use of Scripture, in regard to polity, mainly in its moral or tropological sense. The historical figures of the kings and prophets make occasional appearances not so much as types but as moral exemplars; thus for Barrow, we should imitate David's vigilance at prayer, and for South, our models in temptation ought to include Moses and David.[34]

In the context of their day, the divines' negative warnings about the abuse of Scripture in regard to political matters are as significant as their slight positive applications of it. In all four of the major divines—we have seen Tillotson's—one encounters warnings or questionings about paralleling Old Testament events with contemporary English history. Warning that it is difficult to discern the hand of special providence in history, Barrow writes: "God designs not commonly to exert his hand in a notorious way, but often purposely doth conceal it."[35] In preaching on January 30, 1663, the fourteenth anniversary of the regicide, South rejects "Mystical interpretations of Scripture" woven by "some Apocalyptick Ignoramus or other," and outlines his own method:

No, I pretend not to any such Illuminations. I am neither *Prophet*, nor *Prophetick Prelate*, but account it enough for my Purpose, if I can bring my present Business and the Text together, not by *Design*, but *Accommodation*: and as the words themselves are very apposite and *expressive*, so I doubt not but to find such a Parallel in the Things expressed by them, that it may be a Question, whether the Subject of the Text, or of this *Mournful Day*, may have a better Claim to this *Expression*.[36]

"Accommodation" is a way of reading Scripture, or reading into it, so that it is taken to address a contemporary context for which it was, in fact, not intended.[37] The difference between it and typological reading, for South, seems to be that accommodation does not pretend that the contemporary relevance drawn lies in the "*Design*" of the original author. What South outlines as his practice closely resembles something as simple as Hyde's second type of interpretation of the Psalms. The situations of Israel and England are both "expressive" of the same human emotions and nature; there is no question of a mystical or typological correspondence.

When we speak of the divines' use of the "literal" sense of Scripture to establish theological doctrine, we do not have to distinguish between the intentions of the human and divine authors of the text, between Moses and Paul, for example, and the Holy Spirit who was held to inspire them. South's distinction between "design" and "accommodation," however, shows that the divines distinguished human from divine intentions somewhat more finely when they applied Scripture to political realities. Without explicitly calling attention to the point, the divines tended to assume that, when Scripture is applied to polity, its "literal" sense is that which the human, though still inspired, authors explicitly intended to say to their own political and cultural milieu. They did not deny that the human author, even in this context, writes with divine sanction; the divines merely wanted to avoid the suggestion that these political texts have some hidden, divine meaning unknown to their human authors. Typological readings can thrive only in the gap between human and divine intentions; it was a disputed point whether or not a human author, writing a typological text, fully and prophetically knew what he was doing. Such vagueness of authorial reference was repugnant to the exegetical orderliness of the divines; when writing about political questions in Israel, biblical authors, the divines maintained, should never be thought by "design" also to refer to future political states like England.

In one of his few overtly political sermons, Stillingfleet discussed the problem of possible parallels between the affairs of Israel and England. For a sermon preached to the House of Commons in November 1678, shortly after the murder of Sir Edmund Berry Godfrey, Stillingfleet chose as his text 1 Samuel 12:24–25: "Only fear the Lord, and serve him in truth with all your heart; for consider how great things he hath done for you. But if ye shall do wickedly, ye shall be consumed, both ye and your king." Stillingfleet set up the historical context, that context intentionally addressed by the human author, the disaffection of the Jews with King Saul. But he left the parallel with English affairs to be drawn by his audience. Referring to Moses, Isaiah, Jeremiah, and Ezekiel, he states his main topic: how continuance in sin may cause a nation's ruin. He notes, however, a methodological difficulty: "Here a material question may be asked, whether this connection between their *doing wickedly*, and *being consumed* were not by vertue of that political *Covenant* between God and the people of *Israel* which was peculiar to themselves; and how far it may be just and reasonable to argue the case of other *Nations*, with whom God has entered into no such *Covenant,* as he did with them?" Though Stillingfleet goes on to show how God has intervened in sacred and secular history, and how England itself has received "Wonderfull Mercies and many signal Deliverances from God's hand,"[38] he backs away from the stated problem. One explanation of his reluctance to speak of an English "covenant" is the history of the term in Scotland, with the particularly uncomfortable recollection of Charles II's assumption of the Scots' covenant in the early 1650s. Another explanation lies in the habitual reluctance of the divines to parallel the histories of Israel and England too closely. Stillingfleet's self-consciousness about such parallels led him only to draw the most general conclusions about God's rewards and punishments in regard to national polities.

In a sermon which denies that anomalous behavior in the Old Testament—Abraham's attempted sacrifice of Isaac, Jacob's lie to Isaac, Samson's suicide, and various assassinations—can be a standard of behavior for Christians, South states the general rule for the divines' use of Scripture in political matters: "*The Actions of Persons recorded in Scripture* are not propos'd to us *as Rules of Direction to Live or Act by*: Laws and Precepts are the only things intended for that purpose, and consequently are of an universal Aspect and Obligation, and respect the Actions of all Mankind."[39] The major divines do not appear anywhere specifically to have addressed the problems raised by Filmerite scriptural interpretation; their attitude toward it may be inferred from South's rule. Above all, the literal sense of Scripture must be found and followed. Even when this is established clearly, we may not, without further thought, set up rules for conduct, particularly political conduct, from it. Only scriptural "Laws and Precepts" may be used for this purpose.

South stated his demand for plainness in those scriptural passages which dictate political conduct even more peremptorily than Locke. The most fervently royalist of the divines, South paradoxically resembled, in this demand, Algernon Sidney, who was executed for complicity in an alleged plot against Charles. Arguing from the plain sense of Scripture to political systems and conduct was thus not the unambiguous business so many later seventeenth-century writers made it out to be: even a reliance on the allegedly clear literal and moral sense led, in the real world, to radically different political stances. The resonance of South and Sidney shows that on a broad basis, in the most advanced thought of the day, literalness, whatever its practical eventuality, had superseded allegorical interpretation.

IV

Poetry and verse after 1660 also provide evidence that major writers were taking a colder, harder look at analogical imagery drawn from the Bible. If the minor versifying celebrants of events in Stuart history resorted to typology with abandon, two major poets of the period—Samuel Butler and John Dryden—showed more caution. When typology occurs in *Hudibras*, Butler's cranky masterpiece in three parts (1663, 1664, 1678), it is always satirized. On the one hand, the significant typologizers are Hudibras and his squire, Ralpho, objects of Butler's satire throughout; thus Butler associates typology with the Presbyterian or Independent excess for which Hudibras and Ralpho stand. On the other, Butler's misanthropy aprioristically denigrates any attempt, such as typology makes, to heroicize human conduct. "Butler's language," writes Earl Miner, "presses devaluation on us. He takes from life any pretense to meaningfulness, decency, or beauty."[40] The tactics of devaluation apply to the language of typology in *Hudibras* as to any other idealizing language.

For example, in canto II of the First Part of *Hudibras*, Hudibras castigates a bear-baiting crowd in strongly typological terms. His pompously historical eye interprets bear-baiting as an insult to the idealism of the Good Old Cause. The bear-baiting, Hudibras says, specifically insults the generosity of the Old Cause's supporters, who had brought in their plate, gold, and household wares to melt down into coin and weapons.

Did *Saints* for this bring in their *Plate*,
And crowd as if they came too late?
For when they thought the Cause had need on't,
Happy was he that could be rid on't.
Did they coyn *Piss-pots*, *Bouls*, and *Flaggons*,

Int' Officers of Horse and Draggoons;
And into Pikes and Musketiers
Stamp *Beakers, Cups,* and *Porringers?*
A *Thimble, Bodkin,* and a *Spoon*
Did start up living men, as soon
As in the Furnace they were thrown,
Just like the *Dragons teeth* b'ing sown.
Then was the *Cause* all Gold and Plate,
The *Brethrens* off'rings, consecrate
Like th' *Hebrew-calf,* and down before it
The *Saints* fell prostrate, to adore it.
So say the *Wicked*—and will you
Make that Sarcasmous Scandal true,
By running after Dogs and Bears,
Beasts more unclean than Calves or Steers?[41]

The tactics of devaluation operate on several levels. In his gross language, Hudibras himself ignorantly devalues the original generosity of the Saints. At one point we think that Hudibras has forgotten the meaning of the idolatrous golden calf because he seems to compare the Cause to it; then we learn that this is the version of "the *Wicked*," who say the Presbyterians have made an idol of the cause. Yet Hudibras seems to relish the typological references to Ovid and Exodus for their own sake; as elsewhere, Butler satirizes his excessive rhetoric.

Typology is not a major object of satire in *Hudibras.*[42] One suspects that Butler's occasional devaluation of typology in the poem gains strength from a wider opposition to it in at least some royalist circles; the scarcity of reference makes generalization difficult. Butler's prose works do not provide much help in forming a reliable context for his antitypological stance. Although an attempt has been made to associate Butler's observations on reason and religion with those of the major contemporary divines, isolated remarks of Butler occasionally suggest that he subscribed to a Spinozan rationalism.[43] Butler wrote no sustained prose analysis of reason and revelation or of political typology, as did the divines. With their strained searching for metaphor, Butler's *Prose Observations* are not reasoned essays stating and resolving a problem of fundamental theology. From the poetry and prose we can only gather that he shared some but not all of the points of view of the major divines, and one of these points of view was a bias against the excesses of political typology.

No seventeenth-century poet used political typology as extensively as John Dryden. From *Astraea Redux* (1660) and *Annus Mirabilis* (1667) to "The Secular Masque" (1700), Dryden habitually enriched his heroic treatment of contemporary history by means of types from classical and biblical literature. Moreover, though Dryden cannot be understood as a proponent of patriarchalism, in *MacFlecknoe* (1678) and *Absalom and Achitophel* (1681), the poet shows a special interest in the relation of filiation to succession that parallels the interests of those directly involved in controversy about Filmer's *Patriarcha*, whose first edition appeared in 1680. The precise use of typology in *Absalom and Achitophel* has, however, bothered critical interpreters of Dryden. We may ask whether the thought of the divines about political typology casts any light on Dryden's in 1681.[44]

Dryden's attitudes toward his own typologizing are not always consistent. The heroicization of the king and his sea captains in *Annus Mirabilis* seems serious enough; in the poem Dryden propagandizes England as a chosen nation and its heroes as recurrences of classical and biblical heroes.[45] In such an instance, Dryden seems to take political typology seriously. He does not always do so. The outstanding examples of a debasement of typology occur in *MacFlecknoe*, in which Dryden compares Flecknoe to "Augustus" and Flecknoe tells Shadwell that "*Heywood* and *Shirley* were but Types of thee, / Thou last great Prophet of Tautology."[46] Depending at least on the genre in which an individual poem is written, Dryden feels free to use typology in a straightforward or a debasing manner. In *Absalom and Achitophel* the uses of typology are still more complex. For although Dryden clearly intends to heroicize the king by comparing him to King David, typology at times is debased in the poem.

Recent analysis of the biblical imagery and politics of *Absalom and Achitophel* has tended to show that Dryden is a political moderate in the poem and that a close reading cannot sustain the presumption that the narrator is an arch-Tory.[47] Skepticism about the straightforwardness of

Dryden's typologizing grows in the context of these estimates of his political moderation. I do not mean that Dryden in any way tries to subvert
the authority of the king by means of the poem; rather, he uses typological discourse in it in a somewhat more rational and distant manner than
might a hypothetical true believer in the trappings of Stuart monarchy,
for the narrator of the poem does not stand alone as an employer of typology. Achitophel himself employs it in his temptation of Absalom to
rebellion: he calls Absalom the peoples'

. . . cloudy Pillar, and their guardian Fire:
Their second Moses, whose extended Wand
Divides the Seas, and shews the promis'd Land.

Later in the poem, the people bless Absalom, "their young *Messiah*."[48]

By putting typological imagery into the mouths of the advocates of
"innovation" in the poem, Dryden asks the reader to muse at the distor-
tions that can be made of such language. Indeed, it is paradoxical that the
use of typology by opponents of the king is, in context, serious, whereas
the narrator's own use of typology, as in the lighthearted opening para-
graph about King David's "vigorous warmth," tends not to be so. The
uses of typology in political contexts seem to be not only the medium of
Absalom and Achitophel but also part of its message. To press the point too
closely reduces the delight of Dryden's David-Charles parallel to preaching. Yet one senses that Dryden intended us to understand the typology
of the poem as an ambiguous political tactic—a thing of delight and cele-
bration but not of serious political force.[49] Even the ending of the poem,
it has recently been pointed out, does not employ its comparison of
David-Charles and God the Father with a completely straight face.[50]

Like Tillotson, but without Tillotson's high seriousness, Dryden understood political typology, at least that of his own *Absalom and Achitophel*, as something with "two handles," dependent on "good wit and
strong imagination." Dryden certainly did not learn how to use typology
in a comic fashion from the divines, although there are some adumbra-
tions of its comic possibilities in South. The sources of the brilliance of
the political typology of *Absalom and Achitophel* finally rest in the great-

ness of Dryden's imagination; but this imagination, like Butler's, was freed to work its will by a wider cultural rejection of political excesses and a skepticism about the typological language with which such excesses might be stimulated—a skepticism of which the divines were prominent advocates. This public skepticism about political typology, transformed by Dryden's imagination, is part of the governing wit of the poem.

5

Canon and Text:
The Anglican Model, the New Criticism
of Richard Simon, and Dryden's
Religio Laici

"I n the name of Scripture," the
sixth article of the Thirty-Nine Articles of Religion of 1562 reads, "we do
understand those Canonical Books of the Old and New Testament, of
whose authority was never any doubt in the Church." The article names
thirty-seven books of the Old Testament as canonical, listing several others that may be read for "example of life and manners," if not "to establish any doctrine," and concludes, "All the Books of the New Testament,
as they are commonly received, we do receive, and account them Canonical." The divines of the later seventeenth century more than per-
functorily held and defended this article of the church. The language of
the article reveals the tenor of their rational account of the canon of Scripture. Its verbs—understand, receive, account—provide insight into the
Anglican theory of the canon that obtained throughout the last forty
years of the seventeenth century. The writers of the article and their fellow divines one hundred years later insisted on the passivity of the church
in regard to the canon of Scripture. The church itself does not set up or
institute the canon; it only receives and acknowledges its traditional meaning. The canon makes the church, it is often repeated, not the church the
canon. In regard to the canon, writes Stillingfleet, the church "is but a

Jury of *grand Inquest* to search into matters of *Fact*, and not a *Judge* upon the *Bench* to determine in point of *Law*."[1] Although Anglicans of the later seventeenth century actively defended the truth of Scripture and carefully defined its use in doctrine and polity, the Scripture itself remained in the nature of a gift to them. This gift defined their lives and work; it judged them, not they it. Such a priority governed their theological enterprise; it explicitly governed their theory of the canon of Scripture.

In the later seventeenth century, Anglican understanding of the canon received two main challenges. The first came from Roman Catholicism. Roman Catholics and Anglicans agree, wrote the future bishop of Chester, John Pearson, in 1660, on the books of the New Testament.[2] Neither Anglicans nor Roman Catholics showed great exegetical interest in the contents of those books—including 1 and 2 Esdras, Tobit, Judith, and 1 and 2 Maccabees—which one called apocryphal and the other canonical. Rather, sustained discussion occurred along the line of what makes any book of the Old or New Testament canonical: what authority could one invoke as a principle of canonicity? Roman Catholics argued that a tradition had always existed beside the written tradition of Scripture, a view endorsed by the Council of Trent.[3] We must especially hypothesize an alternate tradition, the Roman Catholic apologists James Mumford and John Sergeant write, when we try to conceive what Scripture might have been in the years of its formation, in the centuries before Moses wrote down the Hebrew history and in the shorter apostolic period before the New Testament as we know it was written.[4] What books are canonical? Are they sufficient for faith? Have their texts been corrupted, even in necessary matters? Have subsequent translations into Greek, Latin, and the vernacular correctly rendered existing Hebrew originals? "Of these, and many more particular Controversies," writes Mumford, "not a word in Scripture."[5] To resolve these problems, one must have recourse to an extrascriptural tradition. In arguing for the existence of such a tradition, Roman Catholic writers often appeared overly eager to destroy the authority of Scripture by pointing out internal problems; such is the pathos of an age of polemics.

Hobbes and Toland presented a second challenge to a specifically Anglican theory of the canon. Hobbes brought evidence to bear that the names of the books of Scripture may not indicate their full authors; on this question the divines were open to difference of opinion. Hobbes also fully accepted the canon of the sixth article: "I can acknowledge no other books of the Old Testament to be Holy Scripture, but those which have been commanded to be acknowledged for such, by the authority of the Church of England."[6] Hobbes's use of "commanded" and "Authority," however, indicates a different degree of emphasis from language used in the sixth article, a difference fully enunciated in his explanation of why the Church of England or any other religious body accepts books as canonical:

By the Books of Holy Scripture, are understood those, which ought to be the *canon*, that is to say, the rules of Christian life. And because all rules of life, which men are in conscience bound to observe, are laws; the question of the Scripture, is the question of what is law throughout all Christendom, both natural, and civil. . . . I have already proved, that sovereigns in their own dominions are the sole legislators; those books only are canonical, that is, law, in every nation, which are established for such by the sovereign authority.[7]

Granting that God's authority is greater than the sovereign's, Hobbes adds: "The question is not of obedience to God, but of *when* and *what* God hath said." Since subjects have no special revelation about this, their reasons must tell them that, to establish peace and justice in this area, as in all others, they must obey the sovereign power. Hobbes's position supports the article and the later divines in that he sees his way clear to accepting the traditional canon. But his formulation of this acceptance destroys the soul of the Anglican position, that the church accepts only what has always been. Hobbes in effect reinforces the Roman Catholic claim for a tradition outside Scripture to verify its canon.

Toland's comments on the canon appear to be destructive. Whether Toland was a skeptic through and through has been debated; his comments on the New Testament canon suggest he was. In his life of John Milton (1698), Toland discusses the problem of the authorship of *Eikon Basilike*. Realizing how disputed the authorship is, Toland writes, "I cease to wonder any longer how so many supposititious pieces under the name of Christ, his Apostles, and other great Persons, should be publish'd and approved in those primitive times."[8] Publicly attacked for this remark, Toland countered in his *Amyntor* (1699) with a list of books allegedly regarded as canonical in the apostolical age, none of which found their way into the accepted canon.[9] He notes that the Council of Laodicaea (364), in whose documents is found one of the earliest full canons, must have enjoyed some special, unrecorded inspiration, to choose a canon from among so many "canonical" books.[10] He impishly concludes with four "curious Disquisitions" for scriptural critics to ponder:

How the immediat Successors and Disciples of the Apostles could so grossly confound the genuin Writings of their Masters, with such as were falsely attributed to them; or since they were in the dark about these Matters so early how came such as follow'd 'em by a better Light; why all those Books which are cited by Clemens and the rest should not be counted equally Authentic; and what stress should be laid on the Testimony of those Fathers, who not only contradict one another, but are often inconsistent with themselves.[11]

Toland's critique did not lead to the affirmation of any tradition that could decide such questions. In his rationalist stance he seemed to have regarded such questions as beneath his attention, as matters only the unenlightened would continue to plod through.

II

Conservative common sense and historical data helped the divines answer challenges to the accepted canon of the Old and New Testament. Such an approach could answer Toland's critique and indeed had, before he wrote. A historical approach could not answer more fundamental critiques such as those of Sergeant and Hobbes. The starting points of the adversaries were so widely distant that meetings on common ground became impossible. It is frustrating to any sense of historical progress to see Sergeant and Stillingfleet advancing the same opposing arguments about the canon in the 1680s as in the 1660s. Neither would back away from his idea of tradition; historical data could not avail in a clash of such armed preconceptions.

What, in more detail, was the Anglican theory of the canon of Scripture? The canon of the New Testament, John Richardson, fellow of Emmanuel College, Cambridge, writes in 1700, involves books "Divine and strictly binding to Obedience, because they were either wrote or confirm'd by the Apostles of our Savior, and we believe that they were so wrote and confirm'd by them not upon the Testimonies of one or two Fathers only, but of the whole Primitive Church, who were capable of Judging in this question." [12] Richardson summarized the thought of the divines on the canon of the New Testament: it was not something created in late antiquity, at a council like Laodicaea; it was not conceived by a group of postapostolical Fathers of the Church, though the universal consent of the Fathers testifies to the canon's existence before and during their ages. The canon always existed, first in the mind of God, then in the minds of its inspired authors, then on paper, authentic copies of which Divine Providence preserves, and then, finally, in the collective mind of the church. The canon the church now recognizes is, in history, the mind of "the whole Primitive Church." It is enough "to establish a Canon to any particular Man," writes the future archbishop of Canterbury, Thomas Tenison, "if he may, by any means attain unto a certain belief, of any Rule, as delivered by Christ; without any superadded Decree Ecclesiastical or Civil." [13] Samuel Parker, bishop of Oxford, writes that "all the Councils in the World can never give Divine Authority to any Book, if it had it not before." [14] According to Chillingworth, the New Testament canon is based on "the Credibilitie of *Universal Tradition*" and, according to Stillingfleet, "the common Tradition of the *Apostolical Churches*." [15]

What is canonical in one age, writes Tillotson, is canonical in all; "no other are the Books which the Ancient Church received for Canonical." [16] "The Authority of those Books is not derived from any Judgment that the Church made concerning them," writes Gilbert Burnet, bishop of Salisbury; "they were writ, either by men who were themselves Apostles of Christ, or by those who were their Assistants and Companions at whose Order, or under whose Direction and Approbation, it was known that they were written and published."[17] Stillingfleet acknowledged that in the early church various heretics called the canonicity of every New Testament book into question.[18] This criticism by no means harms canonicity, to which only the sum of apostolic and postapostolic writers testifies. The early questioning of certain canonical books, such as Revelations, became, for John Edwards, a Cambridgeshire vicar, "a Confirmation of the Truth and Authority of them."[19] That the early church did debate the canonicity of certain books shows its lack of credulity and its awareness that not every early Christian writing was to be accepted as canonical.

The canonicity of the Old Testament books was a more complex problem. Anglicans generally held, with Burnet, that a quotation from an Old Testament book by Jesus or a canonical author of the New Testament rendered that Old Testament book canonical; the books of Moses, the Prophets, and the Psalms especially fit this category.[20] Because of the length of time involved in the composition of the Old Testament, a fully historical scheme is hard to construct. In his first published work, William Lowth wrote that Ezra witnessed to the full Old Testament canon and that the matter was certainly settled by the time of the Septuagint, views with which the divines may be thought to concur. Lowth added that a case could be made for the existence of the canon in Ezra's time more strongly than any arguments against it, a morally probabilistic argument that recurs in the writings of the divines.[21] Stillingfleet argued that, although early Christian services sometimes used noncanonical books, such use did not necessarily argue a universal tradition.[22] Burnet admitted that the canon of the Old Testament may be disordered; yet everything necessary for an "Object of Faith, or a Rule of Life" had been safely conveyed to future generations.[23]

We have seen the commonplace Anglican argument that rational inquiry leads to certainty about the Christian religion as a whole and that once this certainty is reached only the perverse will argue over each and every doctrine. Such a supposition guided Anglican discussion of the Old Testament canon. One must carefully establish historical witness to the canon of the New Testament; this done, only the skeptic would quibble about this or that book of the Old. In recognizing a canon, the divines principally argued against the need for a tradition other than simple commonsense looking at the historical data. If Roman Catholics argue that certain canonical books are lost, writes Stillingfleet, we can hardly look to a church, which lost them in the first place, to restore them.[24]

Because both Roman Catholics and Anglicans of this period admitted that an extrascriptural tradition existed to help one assent to a rightful canon, it is sometimes difficult to distinguish between opposing conceptions of what that tradition might be. In his study of seventeenth-century Roman Catholic theology, George Tavard quotes Abraham Woodhead, an anomalous Roman Catholic fellow of University College, Oxford, after 1660, on the distinction between Roman and Anglican concepts of Scripture. Woodhead wrote that the truly differentiating factor lies in the alternate emphases apologists place on the unlearned reader.[25] From Chillingworth through Stillingfleet, Anglicans maintained that the simplest of believers may understand the plain sense of Scripture on "necessary" matters, that is, those on which one's salvation depends. It was, on the other hand, a constant factor in recusant argument that the unlearned reader cannot reach such an understanding without help from an extrascriptural tradition. Roman Catholic writers habitually amassed data about changing canons and texts to substantiate this point. Learned divines might be able to see the forest from the trees in Scripture, it was argued, but the common reader could not.

Woodhead's distinction about audience is clear. What is harder to clarify is the distinction between various meanings of tradition in the later seventeenth century. Sophisticated Roman Catholic apologists such as Sergeant did not always equate "tradition" with "Pope and Councils." They preferred to argue that, in the face of great uncertainty about Scripture, some other tradition was necessary. Moreover, Anglicans themselves frequently used the term "tradition" in reference to something historical outside of Scripture. As Chillingworth wrote, Scripture cannot decide all controversies concerning itself.[26] As an object of the mind's inquiry, as a definable source of analysis and contrast, this alternate tradition is not easy to grasp. It is certainly not embodied in a pope, in an individual council, or in two or three Fathers of the Church. It is not exactly defined in temporal terms, although the closer the witness was to the apostles, the more worthy the testimony. Perhaps the Anglican view of the very act of understanding Scripture offers the best model for understanding the historical formation of the canon. Reason, applied to Scripture, looking for its plainest meanings, will over a period of time isolate false meanings and hold fast to true ones. Problems will always occur, but the plain, literal sense, with the help of the Holy Spirit, will become clear to the reader who works with patience and humility. So also with the canon: over the first few centuries, the universal church gradually learned, under the guidance of Providence, to distinguish what was truly apostolic from what was not.

Such a model for the recognition of the canon is not a simple one; it says nothing to the clear and distinct ideas Roman Catholic apologists pursued in this area. But it does satisfy the two constant demands Anglicans habitually made for a theory of the canon: that the canon be both apostolic and universal, that is, not the result of some particular faction's prejudice. Perhaps the distinctive Anglican contribution to the discussion of extrascriptural tradition finally rests in a refusal exactly to localize the word of God outside of Scripture, either in a date or set of dates, in a place, or in any distinct, legislative body. As late as 1896, a distinguished Anglican historian of the canon of the New Testament reiterated the sentiment of the divines of the later seventeenth century: "The same Apostolic books as gave life and strength to the early Churches quicken our own. And they are recognized in the same way, by familiar and reverent use, and not by any formal decree."[27]

III

As I have enunciated it, a major Anglican argument for the truth of Scripture directly concerned the credibility of its authors. One might expect, therefore, that the divines developed an extensive theory of how God inspired these authors to express his revelation in human terms. Such is not the case. The divines showed some interest in historical reconstruction of an author's life and times, as evidenced by Stillingfleet's discussion of Moses' education and contemporary reputation. Yet the psychology of the authors of Scripture received little sustained attention. The lessons about human psychology taught by the poets and dramatists of the Restoration are not evidenced in the divines' discussions of the human persons responsible for writing down the scriptural text. Few consistent theories of the psychology of inspiration are extant, and none, so far as I can see, in the writings of Barrow, South, Stillingfleet, and Tillotson. Inspiration clearly was considered a doubtful matter, on which Scripture is vague and which can be understood through a plurality of models—yet a plurality of models is lacking in the period. The problem of inspiration acquires a special acuteness in regard to those books or passages of Scripture whose meaning is recondite, especially various Old Testament prophecies and Revelation. Henry More assigned verbal laxity and ambiguity to the possibility that the Spirit inspired faster than the authors could find words, a somewhat comic situation, though not suggested as such.[28] Taking a safer course, Tillotson held that the Spirit especially inspired authors with arguments that persuade the reader of the truth of doctrine.[29]

If any single description of inspiration may be taken as representative of the broad opinion of the divines, it involves a preference for the plain style: the Holy Spirit inspired authors to write plainly and clearly or, conversely, Scripture that is plain and clear most unambiguously gives evidence of inspiration. The Anglican argument that God would not let salvation depend on ambiguous texts obviously relates to this bias for the plain style. The fullest extant discussion, by Gilbert Burnet, in his commentary on the Thirty-Nine Articles, also accentuates plainness. Burnet distinguishes three scriptural styles and assigns an inspired purpose to each. The plain style takes precedence: God inspired an author to use this style especially on occasions when some law was to be changed. Burnet has passages like the Decalogue and the Sermon on the Mount in mind. So great is the weight of such passages for the welfare of mankind that God would not allow the eccentricities of personal style to make their meaning ambiguous.

A second scriptural style depends less on the action of the Spirit and more on styles relative to the time of composition. This style proposes to excite readers or hearers to an observance of the law. In this category, Burnet places the prophetic books, in which "Many Allusions, Hints, and Forms of Speech must be used that are Lively and Proverbial." The third style gives its audience a clearer or more appealing idea of God; parts of the Bible written in this style include the Psalms, Job, Proverbs, and Ecclesiastes. Withal, inspiration does not necessarily account for "every Tittle" of the words of Scripture but does account for "all that for which we can only suppose that Inspiration was given." We can only suppose that he means by this the "Doctrinal Parts" and "Rule of Life" in Scripture.[30] The New Testament, he writes, is written entirely in the plain style, except for Revelation, written in the second style. Because the New Testament plays such an important role in changing law, one is not surprised at this categorization, however inadequate it may be, at the very least, to some of the more gnomic expressions of Jesus in the Gospels. Burnet's treatment leaves one wondering whether the vagaries of Scripture have been methodized out of existence to fit a preconceived primacy of the plain and simple. Because faith is so rational an act for the divines, an act which assents only to propositions, the divines' appreciation of the imagistic parts of Scripture was not acute. Their respect for the whole of Scripture did not permit them ever to denigrate difficult parts of it; they could not go so far as Spinoza, whose annoyance with historical narrative and prophetic imagery was great precisely because they resist abstraction. Nevertheless, the divines were habitually more relaxed with the plain parts of Scripture, from which doctrines could easily be abstracted for use in controversy.

It should not be doubted that the divines considered all of Scripture inspired. This is clear from a controversy of the 1690s, between Jean LeClerc and William Lowth, a divine whose scriptural studies reached their height only in the next century. In 1690, LeClerc published *Five Letters Concerning the Inspiration of the Holy Scriptures*. LeClerc brought the first two letters forward as if they were not written by himself but by a "Mr. N.," who first became active in an earlier controversy with the French Oratorian, Richard Simon. LeClerc distances himself from his persona: "Tho I said it was hard to answer his Proofs fully, I said not that I was convinced. On the contrary, I propos'd them to the Learned, that I might provoke them to examine the matter carefully, and might draw from their Observations some further Light than my own Meditations could furnish me with." The first two letters explain Mr. N.'s position, which is, in the main, to render minimal those parts of Scripture which are inspired and to stress how much in Scripture is owing to human persons and situations. Mr. N. also writes that inspiration really figures only in the "sense" of Scripture and not in its words and "things." "It is clear, then, in my Judgment that the Things were not inspir'd; nor by consequence the Words; which are less considerable than the Things. It is not certain Terms that are the Rule of our Faith; but a certain Sense."[31] In letters 3 and 4, LeClerc relays N.'s answers to objections; in letter 5, speaking in his own voice, LeClerc attempts a proof of the authority of the New Testament from the character and lives of its authors, without reference to inspiration. As a whole, the letters make up an elaborate game of cat and mouse: the assumption of a persona seems to indicate that LeClerc believed the ideas of the book to be so radical as to necessitate distancing himself from them.

Answering LeClerc's letters in 1692, Lowth says that he had waited for "our Eminent Divines" to respond to LeClerc, and when they did not, began a reply himself, at thirty-two years of age, his first work. Lowth insists that almost all of Scripture is inspired, the traditional position. He not unfairly reduces LeClerc's position to this: that what is "human" is not inspired. Although Lowth grants that some few parts of the New Testament involve explicitly uninspired matter, he says that whenever clearly distinguishing signs are absent, we must presume that the scriptural text is inspired. He sees no reason, as does LeClerc, why authorial collaboration or simple statements of human morality cannot be instances of inspiration. For him, inspiration works in and through the human context. Inspiration resembles the action of God on any created person or thing: "'Tis very hard to Assign just how far Nature goes, or exactly to Define how much Second Causes contribute to the Production of the Effect, and how much is ascribed to God."[32]

On the power of inspiration relative to various scriptural genres, Lowth is vaguer than Burnet. Certainly Saint Paul was inspired, if not in his digressions, at least in his explanation of the mysteries of the Gospels. The eloquence of the proto-martyr Stephen's speech suggests inspiration. In pointing out the ways of Providence in history and in their predictions concerning the Messiah, the prophets were certainly inspired. Prophetic inspiration was local and sporadic, that of the apostles more constant. Lowth offers less a theory of inspiration as sustained objection to LeClerc's simpler, clearer divisions of what is inspired and what is not. Lowth believed that God helped the human authors when they needed help; he also enriched the author who made a special human effort to communicate truth.[33] Inspiration operates in both the plain style and poetic form; the catalyst seems to be the human factor of the author's personality and the needs of his times. Lowth's discussion, unlike LeClerc's, is a posteriori: whatever Scripture is traditionally held to be is inspired, and the rational critic must work backward to understand why. Reason may not dictate what inspiration might or might not be and then divide Scripture up according to its findings. All parts being inspired, we may investigate only how reasonable and necessary each particular instance of inspired writing is. In Lowth's extended treatment of inspiration, we find the habitual Anglican reluctance to allow reason to pin down the limits of how the Spirit may operate in Scripture.

IV

From the writings of the divines it is possible to construct what might be called an existential view of the Anglican common reader of Scripture in the later seventeenth century. This reader, of lesser or greater intelligence, listened at service or read at home the same Scripture, in the authorized version, which he knew was recognized by the primitive church as the word of God. With diligence and humility, under the guidance of the same Spirit who guided the authors, the common reader found no difficulty in apprehending, out of the vast material of Scripture, those few elements which are essential to the Christian faith. Although one hesitates to enumerate them, these essentials certainly include the doctrines of natural religion, set out even in the common notions of Herbert of Cherbury. The reader would also find in Scripture those doctrines which specify his faith as Christian and which more warmly address the human condition: the Trinity, the coming of God as man, the satisfaction paid by Jesus for sin, his bodily resurrection, and the promise of ours. The reader might be hard-pressed to explain some of these doctrines; if he consulted the writings of the divines or heard them preach, he would know that these doctrines are "mysteries." Although they do not insult his intelligence, they reveal something above what his intelligence could reach by itself. Indeed, this is part of the reason why the common reader remained a Christian. But the plain sense of Scripture makes the existence of these mysteries clear.

The Anglican divines of the later seventeenth century did not worry a great deal about the state of the scriptural text in which these mysteries are plainly writ. They tended to regard problems of textual criticism as having been solved, when they occurred, by the Waltons and Lightfoots of their age. In 1667 Thomas Sprat ruefully noted that the great problems in textual criticism had been solved already; he confidently asserted that had they not been, his generation would have been up to the task.[34] In 1683 Thomas Tenison summarized the prevailing optimistic mood concerning the texts used by the English to read the word of God: "The *Learned* know the Originals, and the true ways of Interpretation. And amongst us, those of the Episcopal Clergy have obliged the World with such an Edition of the Bible in many Languages as was not before extant in the *Roman* Church. And a *Romanist* who writes with great mastery in such matters, prefers it before the great Bible of *Paris*."[35] The Romanist of whom Tenison wrote was Richard Simon, whose views of Walton's London Polyglot were not, as we shall see, as simple and positive as Tenison made them out to be. The English could fully trust a church that had produced not only the Polyglot but also the Authorized Version:

We Translate from the Original Tongues, after having compared the Readings of the most Ancient Copies, and of the Fathers: Whilst they [Roman Catholics] Translate the Bible from the *Vulgar Latin*, which, indeed, in the New Testament is a tolerable, but in the Old, a very imperfect Version. If an *English* Bible were turned into any one of the modern tongues by a judicious *Romanist*, who could keep Council, it would pass among many of that Church for a good Catholick Translation.[36]

In regard to both scholarly work on the text of Scripture and the quality of the translation he heard and read, the English common reader of Scripture could rest assured that he possessed as authentic a version of the word of God as possible.

The divines candidly admitted the existence of textual problems that resist facile solution. But the common reader, writes Burnet, need not be bothered with these:

In Fact, we know that there are many various Readings, which might have arisen from the haste and carelessness of the Copiers, from their guessing wrong that which appeared doubtful or imperfect in the Copy, and from a superstitious adhering to some apparent Faults, when they found them in Copies of a Venerable Antiquity. But when all these various Readings are compared together, it appears that as they are inconsiderable, so they do not concern our Faith, nor our Morals; the setting which right was the main end of Revelation.[37]

The doctrine of essentials—that Scripture is plain and clear about matters necessary to salvation—cuts across and, as it were, neutralizes critical findings of variant readings. No divine allowed the possibility that God, having given the Scripture, would permit it to be corrupted in regard to its very purpose as a revelation of faith and morals.

One must add, however, two cautionary footnotes to these confident Anglican declarations. First, neither Tenison nor Burnet, nor indeed any of the major divines were trained in textual criticism. Although their knowledge of ancient languages was often exemplary, their confidence about the text was based on the work of others that was presumed to be definitive. Second, in a most uncharacteristic way, the divines wrote aprioristically when they wrote of the absence of textual corruption in regard to fundamentals. Some doctrinal presupposition that has to be, in these passages, took their minds from their more characteristic, empirical approach to the text.

Almost every Anglican divine who mentioned textual problems in Scripture, or the possibility that some canonical books or passages might have been lost, countered with the doctrine of a providential protection of the text. Such protection underwrites the single, most important theory of why the common reader can trust the text in front of him. Stillingfleet states the thesis heatedly in *Origines Sacrae*:

Can we I say *conceive* that this *God* should so far have *cast* off his *care* of the *world* and the *good* of *mankind* . . . as to suffer any *wicked men*, or *malignant spirits* to *corrupt* or *alter* any of those *Terms* in it, on which mens *eternal salvation* depends: much less wholly to *suppress* and *destroy* it, and to send forth *one* that is *counterfeit* and *suppositious* instead of it. . . ? They who can give the least *entertainment* to so *wild, absurd,* and *irrational* an *imagination* are so far from *reason,* that they are in a good *disposition* to *Atheism*; and next to *suspecting* the *Scriptures* to be *corrupted,* they may rationally *suspect* there is no such thing as a *God* and *providence* in the world; or that the *world* is *governed* by a spirit most *malignant* and *envious* of the *good* of *mankind.*[38]

The argument rests on inference and probability. Given the nature of Scripture as the necessary means to God, God would not allow the absurdity of its corruption. Because of his essence, which is truth itself, God cannot work through absurdities. The argument did not rest, as Stilling-fleet and his contemporaries stated it, on empirical evidence. Its weakness is that it could say very little to a learned critic who bracketed, for the moment, the nature of God and brought full scholarly attention only to the empirical problem of how texts have been corrupted.

Such a critic was the French Oratorian, Richard Simon. Four principal works of Simon appeared in English translation in the 1680s and 1690s: *A Critical History of the Old Testament* (1682), *Critical Enquiries into the Various Editions of the Bible* (1684), *A Critical History of the Text of the New Testament* (1689), and *The Critical History of the Versions of the New Testament* (1692). Throughout these works, Simon invariably focuses on the text itself: first the Hebrew version, when extant, then the Greek, Latin, and, to a lesser degree, vernacular translations. Simon occasionally offers criticism of interpretations of the text; these asides point out the unstable readings on which an eccentric interpretation rests. For example, because of irregular plurals and singulars of Hebrew verbs and nouns, Simon ridicules the use of the beginning of the book of Genesis to prove the existence of the Trinity, "as some Divines have fancy'd."[39] Many such asides occur in the four works, but they do not deter him from his basic project of a critical discussion of manuscripts and published versions of Scripture.

Because Simon's four volumes are filled with textual data about versions of Scripture challenging to the nonspecialist—a problem in the seventeenth century as now—they are not easy reading. Conscious of this difficulty, Simon prefaced the 1682 *Critical History* with a summary of his major findings, listing these under four headings. First, he writes, it is impossible to understand Scripture without knowing the different states of the text at different times and places. This idea resembles Spinoza's insistence on a "history of Scripture," although Simon disagrees with Spinoza elsewhere and exhibits a qualitatively deeper knowledge of scriptural sources than does the *Tractatus*. Second, in a very important and seminal contribution to scriptural interpretation, Simon hypothesizes that "publick Writers," appointed by Moses and the prophets, edited the Old Testament more or less into its present state. These appointed scribes were clearly inspired, Simon believed, when they edited the Old Testament books, "without lessening their Authority, since the Authours of these additions and alterations were real Prophets directed by the Spirit of God." It is difficult to perceive how sincere Simon was in formulating this hypothesis. On the one hand, that he devotes several chapters to it at the start of the *Critical History* suggests that he was serious. The apparatus of the scribal school also permitted him to account, against Spinoza, for the inspiration of the non-Mosaic parts of the Pentateuch.[40] On the other hand, the existence of the scribes allowed Simon to bring up, with undisguised triumph, the many errors they made in transcribing the text and the subsequent ignorance of these on the part of many critics.

Third, the Old Testament as it stands abridges much larger records, which were elsewhere preserved in the Hebrew commonwealth. In making such abridgments, the scribes made at least two types of errors. The "order of these ancient Leaves or Scrolls has not been carefully kept by the Scribes," resulting in "transpositions" that cause problems of continuity in present versions. Also, these scribes failed to edit out, as they moved from larger records to Scripture, unnecessary repetitions, granted the repetitions inherent in Hebrew style. These errors, however, were made not through maliciousness but through simple human carelessness—and by people who were inspired by God. Fourth, the carelessness of the scribes' work has a bearing on seventeenth-century religious controversy: "The great alterations which have happened, as we have shown in the first Book of this Work, to the Copies of the Bible since the first Originals have been lost, utterly destroy the Protestants and Socinians Principle, who consult onely those same Copies of the Bible as we presently have them." Controversies cannot be solved using a vernacular text because it is almost impossible to succeed in translating Scripture: "Those Protestants without doubt are either ignorant or prejudic'd who affirm that the Scripture is plain of it self."[41] Thus Simon argues, on textual grounds, the necessity of an extrascriptural tradition to preserve orthodox dogma.

In the three books of textual criticism that follow the preface, Simon makes other important generalizations that have reference to modes of interpretation as well as textual criticism. Because of the many errors of the scribes, and their inclusion only of "principal Actions" from the larger records, all efforts at composing biblical chronology are fruitless. The search for the perfect manuscript or text must also be abandoned. All translations have their faults, and the originals cannot be adequately reconstructed. Even Origen and Jerome, trying to correct earlier errors, ended up compounding them.[42] Simon distances himself from Roman Catholic narrowness about the Vulgate.[43] We should feel free to move back and forth from translation to translation to deepen our knowledge of Scripture. "This zeal for the Vulgar," he writes, "has chiefly appear'd in *Spain*, where the Inquisition is severe."[44]

In regard to specifically English work in Scripture, Simon had mixed praise for Walton's Polyglot. He liked the 1657 Polyglot's columned format and especially its Greek and Latin texts, more accurate than those in the Parisian Polyglot; he also says that it repeats errors made by the Parisian Polyglot in the Arabic and Syriac texts.[45] Because Walton and his editors tried to distance themselves from sectarian readings, their scholarship was less prejudiced than that of the editors of the Geneva Bible.[46] Simon several times praises James I's proscription of the Geneva Bible, whose texts and marginal notations he considers corrupt. But like all Protestants, the translators of the 1611 version "scarcely acknowledge any other Hebrew Text than that of the *Masoret Jews*, nor any *Greek*, saving that of the Ordinary Copies."[47] Finally, Simon's accumulated analysis of ancient and modern texts continues to attempt to make the *sola Scriptura* an anachronism. No version of Scripture, he repeats, can in itself solve doctrinal difficulties. "Both protestants and Socinians," he writes, "own the Scriptures to be plain and easie to be understood. Wherein they show that they speak only according to the Prejudices of their Religion, and not according to Truth, since they cannot agree upon the Exposition of the chief places upon which they ground their belief."[48]

V

What was the significance of Richard Simon's research for an Anglican of the later seventeenth century? Simon's work specifically challenged Anglican scriptural interpretation in a number of ways. First, Simon's hypothesis of "Publick Writers," who added to and abridged earlier Hebrew records, directly affected the divines' proof of the truth of Scripture from testimony. This proof presupposes that the books of the Old and New Testament were written by individuals whose miraculous works were witnessed by friend and foe alike. The argument is elastic enough to admit that some parts of Scripture, though nothing containing essential doctrine, may not have been written by those whose names they traditionally bear. But this cornerstone of Anglican interpretation cannot support the weight Simon placed on it: the hypothesis that much of the Old Testament was written by scores, perhaps hundreds, of scribes whose names have been lost and of whose actions nothing is known except that they made many errors in transcribing earlier documents. To suggest that Providence oversaw the work of these scribes, given their anonymity and sloppy work, is a hopeless gesture toward legitimacy. For if their existence as "Prophets directed by the Spirit of God" enables Simon to say that the whole Old Testament is inspired, their existence also gives the grounds for saying that many other presumably inspired records have been lost and that what remains may be so confusedly put together as to resist simple interpretation.

Second, Simon consciously evoked the ethos of a critic who was not swayed by sectarian battles but was concerned only with the disinterested truth about the scriptural text. "They who search after truth itself without prejudice," Simon writes, including himself in this number, "value not persons, names, nor their antiquity, especially in things not relating to Faith." Although controversial writers of all ages habitually claim lack of prejudice, Simon's claim has special merit because the body of his writings, in an examination of texts and editions, does not play sectarian favorites. "As for the Writers of our times," he notes, "whether Catholicks or Protestants, I have found none who were wholly free from prejudice," and his practical criticism carries through this observation.[49] Especially in regard to the Vulgate, which he respected but did not hold sacred, his critical work distanced him from those Roman Catholics who were intent on defending papal editorial decisions at whatever cost to disinterested scholarship.

Third, Simon's critical work is massive and convincing, especially in its superb accumulation of empirical data. We may catch the flavor of his attention to detail in a long passage on the calligraphy of medieval scribes:

I have seen a Manuscript which had 24 Books of the Bible, which had been writ at *Perpignan* in the year 1300 in a neat Character; however the Transcriber had put at the end of the letters certain little points for ornaments sake; and this way of adorning of letters, which I have found in some manuscript Copies, has occasion'd much confusion, forasmuch as these little points at top, which incline downwards, are easily mistaken for the letter *Mem*; and *Mem* may easily be taken for *Phe*; *Daleth* for *Heth*, etc. In comparing the Septuagint Translation with the present Hebrew Text, we shall find many of these examples. As in the 19th Chapter of *Joshua* and the 21st Verse, instead of *Seba* as it is in Hebrew, the Septuagint have read in their Copy *Sema* by changing *Beth* into *Mem*. We may ascribe to this way of writing some of the various readings which are called *Keri* and *Cetib*, many of them being caus'd by the changing of *Beth* into *Phe*, *Beth* into *Mem*, *Caph* into *Phe*, etc. . . . . There is another way of writing of Copies which has occasion'd various readings. Some Transcribers at the end of a line huddle the letters so one upon another that it is hard to distinguish *Caph* at the end from a *Vau*; on the contrary, when *Transcribers* have too much room they make the *Vau* bigger, and then it may be taken for *Caph* at the end of a line. . . . . I have observ'd another sort of variety, which proceeds from the Transcribers ruling their Parchment for to write straight, so that the Pen letting down thereupon often changes one letter into another. For example, from the letter *He* a *Mem* may be made, the *He* being closed at the bottom. After the same manner, of a *Resch* or a *Daleth* one may make a *Beth*.[50]

It may be possible, by reference to other manuscripts, to counter such empirical demonstration and the conclusion of textual chaos drawn from it. But to argue with Simon in this way requires, as a base, a lifetime of

familiarity with manuscripts. Locked into arguments about the rationality of Scripture, Anglican divines of Simon's generation rarely possessed
such a background. Controversial theology about fundamental questions
scarcely provided the training ground for the ability to answer Simon in
the only way he could be answered—on empirical grounds.

Last, in his comments directly addressed to Socinian theologians, Simon hardly supports the Socinian way of reading Scripture. Yet he does
insist that a confusion of texts makes Scripture so difficult to interpret
that common readers can scarcely be relied on to find essential doctrine
in it. It is unfair for Simon, in the 1682 work, devoted entirely to the
Old Testament, to generalize on the impossibility of solving Anglican-
Socinian arguments by the *sola Scriptura* principle; for when Anglicans
and Socinians argued about Scripture, the interpretation of New Testament texts was mainly debated, texts excluded by design from the scope
of *A Critical History of the Old Testament*. Simon's later, more conservative
work on the New Testament does not in fact confirm in detail his thesis
about the impossibility of distinguishing, without extrascriptural tradition, between orthodox and heterodox meanings of basic Trinitarian and
christological texts. Nevertheless, Simon's remarks on this problem in
1682 remain challenging for two reasons. First, although the Old Testament was rarely used to show necessary anti-Socinian doctrine, Anglican
divines would not deny that it might hold such; they did not allow themselves to counter Simon's criticisms by saying that the Old Testament is
extraneous to anti-Socinian argument. Second, even if Simon does not
say that specific, major christological texts are corrupt, his methodology
shows how, in the confusion of the manuscripts, they may be so; for the
first time it is possible to fear that the evidence for certain clearly fundamental doctrines may not be clear in Scripture.

Phillip Harth has discussed a number of published Protestant responses to Simon's work of 1682 from the Anglican side. He shows that
they fall into two groups: respondents who thought that the *Critical History* might be a valuable apologetical tool, less its insistence on extrascriptural tradition, and those who regarded it as undermining scriptural authority and encouraging atheism.[51] It is surprising that in this age of
controversy, no major divine published a book or pamphlet devoted to
refuting Simon; notice of his work tends to be in letters or in introduc-

tions to books on other subjects. Publications of far less moment than the 1682 *Critical History* received far more detailed comment and rebuttal from the divines. Presuming the major divines knew of the translation's existence—and Stillingfleet surely did—perhaps they did not reckon the book worthy of a response, though this is hard to believe. It is more likely that, knowing of the book, they simply did not know how to deal with the challenges it presented. A survey of five divines who did comment on it indeed suggests a simple lack of ideas and methodologies to counter to Simon's.

Thomas Tenison, for example, presumably recognized some special worth in the 1682 work; he was anxious to get Simon on his side as a positive evaluator of the English tradition in editing and translating. Tenison achieved this recruitment of Simon only by what seems to be an intentional suppression of evidence. Although all of Simon's criticisms of the Walton Polyglot are not contained in the 1682 *Critical History*, a number are;[52] to find Simon's praise for Walton, Tenison had to disentangle it from negative comment, comment which Tenison ignores when he quotes Simon on Walton in his 1683 work, *A Discourse Concerning a Guide in Matters of Faith*. Tenison's suppression of evidence does not depend on a hope that readers would somehow not find the full text of Simon; this was a public document. Rather, underneath Tenison's suppression of fact lies, I think, the presupposition that the Anglican credentials for scriptural scholarship were so strong that no critic under any scholarly guise whatever could have anything serious to say against them.

In his preface to the first volume of John Lightfoot's *Works* (1684), George Bright encounters Simon in a more critical way than Tenison but shows no evidence that he has grasped the compelling novelty of Simon's arguments and methodology. Bright notes that Rome does not share Simon's open-minded attitudes toward the Vulgate and other translations. He also writes that Simon's criticism of texts and editions is not unique; many similar investigations have also been carried out by "the Protestants, who have not been so forward to publish them, but chose rather to preserve them to longer consideration."[53] Bright offers no examples of such scholarly work. He tries to reduce Simon, against the evidence of much of the 1682 work, to a Roman Catholic apologist for "tradition." Bright ignores Simon's key hypothesis about the schools of public scribes and his conclusions about the impossibility of the perfect text or translation.

John Edwards answered Simon in 1693 in a work dedicated to Simon Patrick, bishop of Ely. Edwards also tried to catch Simon in the snare of tradition. Although he praises Simon as a "great Master of Critical Learning," he thinks the idea of public scribes "founded on no other Bottom than F. *Simon's* Brain"; the idea is forwarded "to depreciate the Bible, and to represent it as a Book of Fragments and Shreds" and to make the reader rest on "Tradition." It is difficult to understand in what Simon's critical mastery consists, if not in the findings that lead him to hypothesize a multiauthored Pentateuch. Like Tenison, Edwards refuses to admit that the divines' schemes of scriptural proof need emendation because of Simon. "Notwithstanding then the Cavils and Objections of designing Men," Edwards writes, "we have reason to believe and avouch the Authority of the Old Testament, and to be thorowly perswaded that the Books are entirely transmitted to us without any Corruption, and are the same that ever they were, without any Diminution or Addition."[54] The "reason" of which Edwards writes involves, presumably, the a priori arguments from authority traditionally formulated by the divines; Edwards does not understand the radically text-oriented methodology that Simon introduces.

In another introduction to a larger work, the 1692 rebuttal of LeClerc's theory of inspiration, William Lowth in part defends Simon; this is because two of his own adversaries, LeClerc and John Dryden, are also Simon's. Lowth says that LeClerc and Dryden misrepresent Simon, an argument which itself involves misrepresentation of Dryden's *Religio Laici*; Lowth seems to be angry with Dryden for his change of religion and his appearance to the world, after 1685, as a Roman Catholic apologist. Mentioning Simon's theory of public scribes but then avoiding discussion of it, Lowth, like Edwards and Bright, tries to characterize Simon as a stereotype of Roman Catholic thought about extrascriptural tradition. Simon, writes Lowth, "has taken a great deal of Pains to weaken the Authority of the Scripture text on purpose to set up the Certainty of Tradition in its place"; Simon thereby curries favor with his ecclesiastical superiors, who might otherwise object to his work.[55] Although there may be a canny truth in Lowth's surmise, he ignores Simon's impartiality about Roman scriptural criticism as a whole. As did Edwards, Lowth recognized a certain greatness in Simon but was curiously unable to locate it in some general truth enunciated by the *Critical History*. The same ambivalence is evident in both authors: the novel importance of Simon's work is granted, but in the course of argument this novelty is reduced to something hackneyed and refuted with the old arguments against nonwritten tradition and in favor of the providential protection of the text that are amply undermined by Simon himself.

One divine who did seem fully to understand that at least one of Simon's conclusions—the school of public scribes—directly challenged the Anglican way of reading Scripture was Edward Stillingfleet. In an unpublished sermon, delivered February 23, 1683, at Whitehall, Stillingfleet asked the key questions, from the Anglican point of view, about Simon's hypothesis:

For what Divine Assistance could these Men have, who were guilty of so many faults in their own Copies? For either the charge against the present Copies is true or false; if it be true, as is pretended, what blasphemy is it to charge so much disorder & Confusion, so many interpolations & repetitions on the Holy Spirit of God? Besides, what assurance can we have of anything like Divine Inspiration in these Publick Writers, who preserved the Originals in the Sacred Registeries & gave out imperfect Copies? We read of no Miracles they wrought, no Prophecies of theirs accomplished, no Testimony given to them by other Prophets?[56]

Stillingfleet perfectly grasped Simon's argument when, if true, the argument challenges the proof of scriptural truth from authority.

In answer to Simon, Stillingfleet argues that if such erroneous copies of the books of Moses ever existed, they did so by the time of Christ. Yet Jesus and the Apostles not only quote the Pentateuch but refer to it explicitly as Moses' work.[57] Could Jesus, the Son of God, have been in error? Thus Stillingfleet sweeps aside, again from the a priori point of view, Simon's careful research into the state of the text at different times in history. The Mosaic authorship is true because Jesus noticed it; the hypothesis of the scribes and the fact of textual problems are not true because Jesus did not mention them. Stillingfleet realized the importance of one of Simon's cardinal suggestions and attempted to counter it; but he did not grasp the importance of the methodology of textual criticism that led Simon to that conclusion. Irène Simon has noted the "Church of England's resistance to historical and philological scholarship" after 1660.[58] Such resistance is certainly not evident in discussions of the canon of Scripture; in answering Toland or various Roman Catholic critics, the divines were capable of summoning respectable historical evidence. In response to Richard Simon, however, they were unable or unwilling to do so. They refused to enter the empirical ground he cleared.

VI

If the Anglican divines were unwilling or unable to encounter Richard Simon on his own ground in the 1680s, two prominent Anglican laymen of the time were not: John Locke and John Dryden. Neither Locke nor Dryden constructed a definitive response to Simon; but both exhibited an awareness that the critical evidence he amassed challenged the traditional way Anglicans discussed the truth of Scripture. Through his extensive correspondence with French and Dutch friends, Locke came to know the controversy Simon's work caused on the Continent.[59] Locke also carefully read an original French edition of *A Critical History of the Old Testament*; a notebook preserved in the Lovelace collection at the Bodleian Library contains summaries of and quotations from Simon's first major critical work. At the start of the notebook, Locke summarizes the internal logic that led Simon to hypothesize his school of scribes:

pere Simon brings proofs and instances
1° That the severall books of the OT are collections and epitomes of other writings more ancient
2° That in them there are severall things omitted
3° Severall things added
4° Severall repetitions
5° Several varietys
To solve this he supposes that there were publique officers In the commonwealth from Moses his time downwards

Locke adds that these writers' business was to write and register current history, to make collections of and publish such records, and "to omit add or alter what they thought fit or served their present purpose"; these authors were called "prophets" before the captivity and "scribes" after, and they were inspired.[60]

If Locke's notes seem merely a summary of certain early pages in Simon's work, the divines seemed incapable of making even such a bland summary. For Locke perceived what the divines did not: both the centrality of the hypothesis of the scribes to Simon's work and the reason for the hypothesis. That is, Simon did not suggest the existence of "publique officers" in order to downgrade written tradition or lead his readers to Roman Catholicism; rather, he believed that the scribes "solved" problems posed by the "proofs and instances" of omissions and alterations found in an empirical analysis of the text. Locke's notes assume that Simon was a scientist who amassed new empirical data and sought a simple way to explain their existence. We know from many other of his writings that Locke believed in the *sola Scriptura*; the argument from testimony is a cornerstone of his scriptural theology. But such allegiances did not prevent him from fairly estimating the scientific impartiality which Simon claims.

John Dryden's encounter with the *Critical History* is, unlike Locke's, recorded in a public, signed document of 1682, *Religio Laici; or A Laymans Faith*. Recent commentary has shown that *Religio Laici* is an "Anglican" poem; that is, both its first half, on deism, and its second, on Simon, extensively and at times verbally borrow their theological ideas from the writings of the Anglican divines of the period.[61] Insofar as this dependence influenced the second half of the poem, the dependence is a reiteration of the cardinal Anglican tenet about providential protection of the text of Scripture: that God would never allow the text to become corrupt in regard to fundamentals:

More Safe, and much more modest 'tis, to say
God wou'd not leave Mankind without a way:
And that the *Scriptures*, though not *every where*
Free from Corruption, or intire, or clear,

Are uncorrupt, sufficient, clear, intire,
In *all* things which our needful *Faith* require.[62]

Thus, like the divines, Dryden insists that the field of battle with Simon
must be drawn not on empirical grounds but on the presupposition that
God, to whose goodness all of Scripture testifies, would not leave mankind without a way to him. Though the development of ideas in the second half of *Religio Laici* is complex, recent commentary is undoubtedly
correct in showing that the argument from Providence forms Dryden's
principal, repeated counter to Simon.

Simon's preface posed a problem that could not be answered with any
arguments proposed by the divines Dryden had read. How should an
Anglican confront the thesis that so great are the textual problems in
Scripture that even "things which our needfull *Faith* require" are not
clearly present in the text? For Dryden and the divines, such necessary
doctrine certainly included the divinity of Jesus. Dryden admits a Simonian antagonist into the dialectic of the poem who presses this point:

Are there not many points, some needfull sure
To saving Faith, that Scripture leaves obscure?
Which every Sect will wrest a several way
(For what *one* Sect Interprets, *all* Sects *may*:)
We hold, and say we prove from Scripture plain,
That *Christ* is GOD; the bold *Socinian*
From the *same* Scripture urges he's but MAN.
Now what Appeal can end th' important Suit?
Both parts *talk* loudly, but the *Rule* is *mute*.[63]

The discussion has passed beyond the distinction between necessary and
unnecessary matters in Scripture. Dryden lets the Simonian antagonist
center in on one clearly necessary doctrine, the divinity of Jesus. Dryden
opens a chasm that Anglican distinctions, having been bypassed, cannot
fill. The status of the argument shifts from the Providence of God to the
empiricism of textual study, as Simon himself had focused this empiricism on the Socinian question in the preface to the *Critical History*.

Dryden does not in fact answer the Simonian antagonist in the poem. Instead of addressing the problem of whether the "*Rule*" of Scripture is mute, the narrator of the poem moves, immediately after the above passage, to a self-effacement of himself as a simple and honest layman who notes that many are saved "who never heard this Question brought in play." [64] He displaces the critical and theological question onto the grounds of popular religion. The "Anglican" poem moves firmly on. The steadily sensible tone of *Religio Laici*—both its medium and its message—continues to govern the whole. I do not think we can say that Dryden tries to subvert the Anglican doctrine of providential protection of the text. Rather, his inability to solve the problem does not prevent him from letting the problem be posed; the "honest Layman" is tripped, for the moment, by his own honesty. As G. Douglas Atkins writes, this section of *Religio Laici* shows "Dryden's failure, indeed powerlessness, to deny that even such passages in Scripture as those treating of Christ's nature are obscure." [65] The poem as a whole does not suffer from anxiety over this failure, which is a failure also in the theological sources Dryden calls on throughout; the carefully controlled dialectic of *Religio Laici* of its nature allows for both the registering of real opposition to its Anglican thesis and the integration of opposition into a greater, more placid totality. The Simonian objection, however, is not and cannot be answered inside the theological framework Dryden assumes. It is rhetoric alone and not successful counterargument that allows the poem to move on.

A second passage suggesting Dryden's apprehension concerning Simon's achievement occurs earlier in the second half of the poem. Dryden writes of the inferences one draws from reading Simon:

If *Scripture*, though deriv'd from *heaven'ly birth*,
Has been but carelessly preserv'd on *Earth*;
If *God's own people*, who of *God* before
Knew what we know, and had been promis'd more,
In fuller Terms of Heaven's assisting Care,
And who did neither *Time*, nor *Study* spare
To keep this Book, *untainted*, *unperplext*;
Let in gross *Errours* to corrupt the *Text*:
Omitted *paragraphs*, embroyl'd the *Sense*;

With vain *Traditions* stopt the gaping Fence,
Which every common hand pull'd up with ease:
What Safety from such *brush-wood helps* as these?[66]

The passage is difficult to read because of the extended protases of Dryden's conditional sentence. The whole seems uttered not by the Simonian objector but by the Anglican narrator of the rest of the poem: do the "ifs" of this passage register matters of fact, or allegations of some implied Simonian, brought in for the moment without warning? That the apodosis does not deny the allegations and that the protases have such disproportionate weight make the affirmation of the whole ambiguous indeed. We might expect a denial that Scripture is in such a state; instead we are led off again to Roman Catholic tradition, a red herring at this syntactical point.

As Harth notes, Dryden "completely misunderstood what the French priest [Simon] meant by tradition."[67] Dryden assumed "tradition" was merely oral, a view he revises in *The Hind and the Panther*, having by 1687 read more widely in Roman Catholic apologetics. Nevertheless, Dryden's full estimate in 1682 of a Simonian model of Scripture, with its gross errors and omitted paragraphs, is left standing intact. Again Dryden is too honest to ignore what Simon has done and too uncertain of an answer to deal with it adequately. No one in 1682 could in fact deal with Simon; one cannot blame Dryden for backing away from an impossible task. Awareness of the problem and backing away from it through rhetorical cleverness—into this nexus fear of a Simonian-Socinian critique later fits. Reading sensitively we may catch Dryden in an awareness of a major change in the way intelligent believers will have to read Scripture. However Dryden implements standard Anglican apologetics about Scripture and its text in *Religio Laici*, he also has become aware that problems have arisen for which those apologetics do not provide an answer.

Neither John Locke nor John Dryden provides convincing counterarguments to Simon's estimate of the confused state of the Old Testament text, his hypothesis of a school of scribes, or his suggestion that key doctrinal questions cannot be solved on the basis of the text of Scripture. Perhaps Locke never intended to do so. The only way really to refute Simon was to find alternate traditions and readings that might substantiate different conclusions; though learned in their own ways, Locke and Dryden were not adept at such critical work. In the context of the divines' writing about Simon, Locke and Dryden's achievement is not one of apologetics but of openness to the new empirical methods Simon introduced. Both tactically controlled this openness—Locke by writing in his private notebooks, Dryden in the dialectical structure of a complex poem. Yet in their contributions to the debate over the *Critical History of the Old Testament*, one senses true and unique doubt that, after Simon's work, the foundations of the Anglican way of reading Scripture still stood firm.

John Dryden, by Godfrey Kneller. Reprinted by permission of the Trustees of the National Portrait Gallery, London.

Edward Stillingfleet, by Mary Beale. Reprinted by permission of the Master and Fellows of St. John's College, Cambridge.

John Tillotson, after Kneller. Reprinted by permission of the Trustees of the National Portrait Gallery, London.

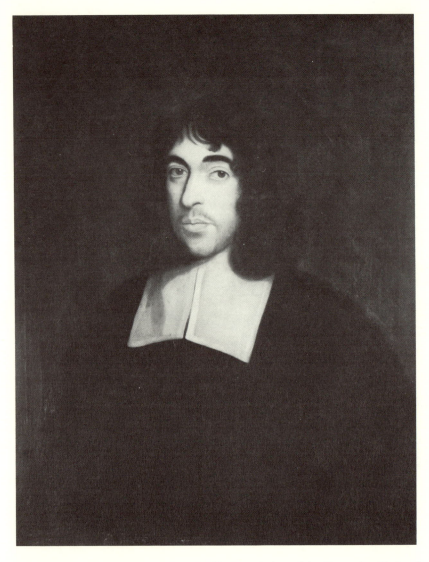

Robert South, artist unknown. Reprinted by permission of the Governing Body of Christ Church, Oxford.

6

The Socinians and Locke

$\mathbb{I}$n the controversial literature of the later seventeenth century in England, the term "Socinian" has at least two separate, if allied, meanings. From the point of view of doctrine, writers were "Socinian" in that they followed all or part of the teachings of Fausto Paolo Sozzini (1539–1604), or Socinus. Socinianism thus used implies a rationalist scriptural interpretation; the accordance to Jesus of a high place in the divine order but not of divinity; the limiting of Jesus' role in the drama of human redemption principally to one of moral exemplarity; the maintenance of minor heterodox doctrines such as mortalism; and the advocacy of a wide tolerance for believers of all creeds. Even in this meaning of the term, however, seventeenth-century usage is not always exact. Some writers who held to much of what Socinus taught denied at times that they were Socinian, for the term may be thought to imply a theological position outside the mainstream of Christianity. For a similar reason, in the last decade of the century, writers who maintained one or more of Socinus's teachings began to call themselves "Unitarians," attempting to accent not the heterodoxy of their theology but its fidelity to unquestionably scriptural teaching concerning the unity of God. Some Socinians in England left the established church; more often it appears that they did not.[1] As a set of doctrines, Socinianism is thus a sixteenth- and seventeenth-century reappearance of the subordinationist side of the controversies that occurred in the church of antiquity; in its many forms, subordinationism challenged the nature of God as three-in-one and subordinated the role and nature of Jesus and the Holy Spirit to the Father's uniqueness.

The second meaning of "Socinian" in the period is more difficult to define clearly. The term often characterizes a methodology that, for those who used it, places a greater accent on human reason than is proper in the delicate balance between the reason of the interpreter and the fullness of scriptural revelation. Taken thus, the term may apply to those who actually held Socinian doctrines; it may also be used of those who did not hold them, and even attacked them, who in some way accentuated reason to a degree thought unorthodox by others. As an index of methodology, the term is impossibly vague, as is noted by such recent commentators as Irène Simon and John Redwood.[2] Some Roman Catholics and Anglican high churchmen resolutely muddied the waters on this point. As Gilbert Burnet writes of the "Latitudinarians": "The making out of the reason of things being a main point of their studies, their enemies called them Socinians."[3] Several writers—Hyde, Glanvill, and the Cambridge Platonist Henry Hallywell—clearly felt the need to protect themselves against such criticism.[4] The differences between the methodologies of the major divines and the Socinians are, without reference to the doctrines evinced through those methodologies, not easy to locate. Indeed, any characterization of these divines as Socinian prompts a renewed effort of establishing how "reason" and "Scripture" are, in their theological projects, opposed or allied. Barrow, South, Stillingfleet, and Tillotson argued with Socinian doctrine and methodology throughout their careers; South especially showed, in his arguments against them, a knowledge of the particularities of Socinian thought.[5] In the 1690s, South, Stillingfleet, and Tillotson turned to anti-Socinian apologetics with renewed interest.

II

The immediate cause of this restored interest in Socinian theology was three collections of tracts published between 1691 and 1695: *The Faith of One God* (1691), *A Second Collection of Tracts, Proving the God and Father of Our Lord Jesus Christ the Only True God* (1693), and *A Third Collection* (1695). Bibliographers have been able to assign a number of tracts to Stephen Nye, an Anglican rector in Hertfordshire from 1679 to 1719; a few tracts in *The Faith of One God* are expressly attributed to John Bidle (1615–62), the "Father" of the English Socinians.[6] As published, almost all of the twenty-nine tracts that make up the three collections are anonymous. A clandestine atmosphere envelops the whole: the place of publication is usually missing from the tracts' title pages, when title pages are there at all; not all the tracts are dated. Since most of the tracts were written and published over a four-year span, it is not surprising to find a marked consistency of opinion in them. This consistency is especially evident in the rules for scriptural interpretation that the tracts as a whole enunciate and that will, if followed, show that the meaning of Scripture is Socinian. These rules are occasionally but not always stated in the abstract; they emerge as the Socinian tractarians reinterpret Old and New Testament texts commonly held to prove the preexistence of the Logos and the divinity of Jesus.

In the tracts dealing with scriptural texts, Socinian interpretation is literal. It insists that the meaning of Scripture, especially of the New Testament, is clear and plain: "The Gospel being plain and easy in all necessary points both of faith and Manners; there is no need of great Abilities, or of Learning, but only of Sincerity and a free unprejudiced Mind, to judge truly and to choose safely."[7] The tractarians are keen to demonstrate that there are no "mysteries" in the Gospels: "The Holy Ghost's Intent was not to make us Philosophers, he always accommodates himself to our most common Ideas, and the Expressions of Scripture, which seem to have occasioned the Notion of a Mystery, are only Figures and Expressions common either to our Stile, or the time wherein it was written."[8] The intellectual pilgrimage of John Bidle, as narrated in *The Faith of One God*, illustrates the Socinians' claim that the literal meaning of Scripture is not Trinitarian: in the account, Bidle comes to Socinian theology not by reading scriptural commentaries, not even those of Socinus, but by reading the Scriptures themselves without prejudice.[9] Anyone who does this, the tracts argue, will find Scripture to be "Unitarian," a term the tracts made widely popular for the first time: "The Revelation [of God's unity] made to us in holy Scripture is Categorical, Apodictical, Express, and Direct."[10]

If the unprejudiced reader encounters difficulty with an individual,

disputed passage of Scripture, the tractarians offer three practical helps.
The first is the whole of Scripture, especially those passages which lu-
cidly teach the unity of the Judeo-Christian God: "Let our opposers show
a Reason why they decline an Interpretation which the Scripture itself af-
fords to us, and how it comes to be Heresy, to understand the meaning of
one Text, by the help of such other Texts as are confest to be clear and
evident?"[11] The second help is simply a good knowledge of the biblical
languages, especially Greek; the tractarians often examine New Testament phrases in the original to show how they ought not be construed to
maintain Trinitarian doctrine. Pagan, Greek usages of relevant vocabu-
lary and grammatical construction occasionally assist this project.[12] The
Fathers of the Church of the first three centuries form the third interpretive help; the Socinians maintain that these Fathers did not teach the
Trinity, and some of the tracts are devoted to assembling data on this
point.[13] Through this third practical help, the Socinians make an obvious
plea against the charge of innovation often brought against them. Finding
Unitarianism in the early Fathers allows the Socinians to say that it is they,
not the Trinitarian theologians, who maintain the oldest and most authentic traditions of the church. With these three aids, the Socinian tractarians find the literal meaning of Scripture to be Unitarian.

A number of the tracts deal not with Scripture but with philosophical
analyses of the terms that Trinitarians impose on Scripture. It is frequently maintained that the doctrine of the Trinity is absurd; in their various attempts to establish the principle of three-in-one, Trinitarian theologians violate the laws of reason, in a narrow sense, which cannot cope
with such contradiction of basic notions. The tracts carefully maintain,
however, that, should a conflict between Scripture and reason arise, their
primary allegiance is to Scripture. Socinians "always prefer the infinite
Wisdom of God, before the infallible Dictates of Humane, or Angelick
Reason."[14] The language of the tracts is not always unambiguous on this
point, but when their writers squarely face the point, they carefully insist
on the primacy of Scripture. They do this because they wish to maintain
themselves solidly inside the Judeo-Christian tradition, especially as it
was enunciated in seventeenth-century Protestant theology. Also, the
tractarians wish to distance themselves from all theologians in the tradition of Athanasius, whose creed forms the object of special Socinian

abhorrence, as a clear example of a complex Platonic overlay on what is essentially simple, scriptural doctrine. In the 1690s, William Sherlock engaged in a particularly involved controversy with South about "person" in the Trinity; Sherlock, whom South accused of tritheism, comes in for occasional satire, throughout the tracts, as a metaphysical speculator gone wild.[15]

If reason and Scripture seem to conflict in the interpretation of a given passage, the Socinians search for a meaning to the text that will conform to reason.[16] They resolve the conflict, in the main, by identifying metaphors in the literal sense and interpreting them accordingly—that is, by making the meaning of the metaphor, the *significatum*, the basis for doctrine, not the metaphor itself, the *significans*. Thus "the most Direct and Ample Expressions, that imply (if taken in their more usual Signification) an impossible Sense or Doctrine, or an Absurd and Contradictory, must be understood as spoken and intended *Figuratively*, and this not only in Scripture but in all other Writings and Writers."[17] The tractarians echo LeClerc's language on inspiration, but with a different emphasis: "The Word of God does not consist in meer Words, the Things chiefly are inspired, not so much the Terms, wherein Men do, to no purpose, seek for Mysteries."[18]

Why is it necessary to identify and rationalize scriptural metaphors? How did it come about that New Testament authors wrote, from a seventeenth-century point of view, so imprecisely? The very unanimity of Scripture on the unity of God allowed the inspired authors to drop their guard, as it were. Because these authors so assumed God's unity, they occasionally carelessly used language that might suggest Jesus' divinity or preexistence.[19] Only after the first three centuries did overreaching metaphysicians begin to lose the common sense of God's unity and interpret biblical metaphors attributing indisputably high power to Jesus as proof of his place as an eternal equal to the Father. Just as one does not maintain that Jesus is literally a vine or a road, so one must not maintain, when Scripture says that Jesus sits at God's right hand or is his firstborn, that the phrases substantially qualify the unity of God taught unambiguously everywhere in Scripture.

Finally, the Socinian tracts fulfill the anxiety, adumbrated in Dryden's *Religio Laici* ten years before, that Socinians might press the new textual criticism into service. Again and again, the tracts argue that the Unitarian texts of Scripture are incorruptible and that key Trinitarian texts rest on faulty copies, imperfect translations, and purposeful tampering with manuscripts by Trinitarian scribes: "How long, do they think, will it secure their Cause; that they combat us with Texts, either wholly of their own Devising, and unknown to the Antients, or grossly, and notionally perverted in the Translation of them?"[20] The standard Unitarian texts exist "in all Copies both of the Hebrew and the Greek, and can no other ways be *rendred* from the Original Text; or more clearly thus, as to these Texts, there is no *Variety* or *Difference*, in the *reading*, in the Copies of the *Original*, or any *Uncertainty* in the *Translations* of those Copies."[21] Although this textual emphasis can already be seen in the work of Bidle, who questions the authenticity of 1 John 5:7, of clearly Trinitarian wording, on textual grounds,[22] Socinian higher criticism comes into its own in the tracts written in the 1690s. The work of Richard Simon, mentioned only once in the tracts,[23] had taken effect. It is probable that these tracts exhibit the first successful integration of modern textual scholarship in Scripture into a sustained theological project.

From the point of view of Anglican scriptural interpretation in the later seventeenth century, the Socinian interpretation of the 1690s contains much that is traditional, especially in its assumption that the saving truths of Scripture are contained in the literal sense alone. The average reader can reach these saving truths without external aid; with only slight modification, the tracts also maintain this common assumption of the divines. More than one tractarian denies that he belongs to any special sect—Papist, Lutheran, Calvinist, even Socinian. "I am a Christian, I thank God," one writes. "I side only with Truth."[24] On the other hand, the methodology of the tractarians is not as traditional as they attempt to make it appear. Unlike the divines, the tractarians admit that a situation might exist in which the literal meaning of Scripture may conflict with what reason allows as possible. This situation admitted, the unity of the truth from two sources given by God, Scripture and reason, is questionable. Moreover, for all their pious insistence on the primacy of Scripture, it is always the Scripture which is corrected when a conflict between it and reason occurs. Either it is found that a text can be emended on the basis of a survey of ancient copies, or the interpreter realizes, under the pressure of the conflict, that the text at issue uses metaphorical language. The compromise always occurs on Scripture's ground, not reason's.

III

Perhaps the closeness of some of the tractarians' methodological presuppositions to the divines' own partly caused the promptness and seriousness of the divines' response. These poorly printed tracts, whose title pages, when they exist, reveal no authors, were openly and lengthily attacked by major churchmen in major pulpits, including both Westminster Abbey and Whitehall. Stillingfleet himself was conscious of the prospect of overreaction. He noted that if Trinitarians did not respond to the tracts, their authors would think the divines fearful; if Trinitarians did respond, they would run the risk of blowing the significance of the tracts out of proportion.[25] Yet sooner or later, the divines must encounter the Socinian problem in some detail. Richard Simon's charge was too close to the truth to be ignored: that Protestant Trinitarians and Socinians use the same interpretive principles and arrive at conflicting conclusions and that there is, therefore, something wrong with those principles.

South contributed to the debate in only one sermon, "Christianity Mysterious and the Wisdom of God in Making It So," delivered in Westminster Abbey on April 29, 1694. South reduced the Socinian position to an antiscriptural rationalism. The Socinians, he charged, refuse to accept the simple fact that the human mind is inherently limited. For South, "mystery," or the rationally incomprehensible, is a necessary, desirable, and permanent quality of scriptural revelation. The Socinian starting point, as South interprets it, that reason is the measure of revelation, is a sophistry; from the tracts, one learns "the gross *Unreasonableness*, and the manifest Sophistry of mens making whatsoever they find by themselves *not Intelligible* (that is to say, *by Human Reason not Comprehensible*) the measure whereby they would conclude the same to be *Impossible*."[26] This tactic is the "main hinge" on which all Socinian arguments turn. Socinians suppose that they can do away with human fallibility and rational weakness. The tracts and their methods resemble "*Infallible Cures*, which we daily see posted up in every corner of the Streets." But human ignorance, like sickness and death, is always with us. Both quack cures and the Socinian tracts are "always very large in Pretence and Promise, but short in Performance, and generally Fatal in their Practice."[27]

Other than saying that the words of Scripture and the "constant, universal sense of all Antiquity" confirm the mysteries of the Trinity and Incarnation, South refused to encounter the many Socinian arguments about the plain sense of Scripture being Unitarian. He avoided argument about this or that problem text. Instead, he countered the principle of the unlearned reader with that of a special order in the church, whose function it is to study the Scriptures professionally, with the skills learned in the universities, "the standing Nurseries of the Church." "God has appointed a certain Order of Men to declare, and dispense these *Mysteries.*" Anglicans need not have "Implicit Faith" in this order, for that is Romish practice, but simply "Due Deference, and Submission."[28] This distinction between implicit faith and due submission seems to be a very fine one, and South does not linger to enlarge upon it. Avoiding the Scylla of Socinus, he veers close to the Charybdis of Catholicism, even as he denies movement in that direction. In candidly asserting the need for learning to read Scripture, South is consistent with earlier statements he had made about the necessity of learned clergy. Nevertheless, the precise issue seems to have eluded him: to undergird, on Protestant principles, in a restatement of the *sola Scriptura*, the doctrines denied by the tracts.

Tillotson responded at length to the three main items on the Socinian agenda: the Trinity, the divinity of Jesus, and the real nature of the satisfaction paid by Jesus for the sins of mankind. In 1693, he preached and published "A Sermon . . . Concerning the Sacrifice and Satisfaction of Christ" and "A Sermon Concerning the Unity of the Divine Nature and the B. Trinity," the former before the queen at Whitehall; in the same year he published *Sermons Concerning the Divinity and Incarnation of our Blessed Saviour.* The volume contains four anti-Socinian sermons delivered in 1679 and 1680 at St. Lawrence Jewry, "now revised and enlarged by the Authour" to answer "the importunate clamours and malicious calumnies of Others" against him.[29] Nonjuring clergy had questioned Tillotson's orthodoxy, in charges that seem to have less to do with what doctrines Tillotson held than with what oaths he had taken, after 1688, to the new monarch, as well as with his attempts at wider comprehension for the church; the publication of the sermons did nothing to stop the controversy, which continued after the archbishop's death in 1694.[30] Contemporary accounts of Tillotson often stress his gentle and kindly nature. He tempers his attack on the Socinian tractarians with praise for their "fair way of disputing and debating matters of Religion without heat and unseemly reflections upon their Adversaries."[31] Such respect for Socinian fairness, however, did not prevent Tillotson from a vigorous attack on their methodology and conclusions.

Aside from the political context and the attacks of nonjurors, why was Tillotson thought to be allied with the Socinians? He was friendly with Thomas Firmin, a philanthropist who sponsored the Socinian tracts, and he is referred to favorably in them, for his "sound Learning and wondrous Modesty."[32] In his last letter, late in 1694, he wrote of the Athanasian Creed, "I wish we were well rid of it."[33] Moreover, Tillotson's clearly anti-Socinian sermons of the 1690s repeatedly express disdain for the overlay of Platonic terms some had placed on the simplicity of Scripture. Of the "hypostatic union," he writes: "It is not safe for our shallow understandings to wade further than the *Scripture* goes before us, for fear we go out of our depth and lose our selves in the profound inquiry into the deep things of God."[34] Tillotson clearly regards some Trinitarian theology as overreaching what the human mind can do; in this belief, he agrees with a common Socinian complaint. Yet Tillotson sees no reason why the terms "Person" and "satisfaction" for Jesus' place in the Trinity and his role in redemption cannot be used to describe scriptural realities;[35] this view puts him in direct opposition to the tracts. Thus, although Tillotson's general position is against the tracts, he makes occasional gestures toward them, their authors, and their sponsors that could be interpreted, by those opposed to him on political grounds, as pro-Socinian.

The key to understanding Tillotson's thought in the midst of the Socinian controversy of the 1690s is his lifelong commitment to the integrity of Scripture. Whatever is in Scripture must be believed as the truth of God: "A man must not deny what God says, to be true; though he cannot comprehend many things which God says: as particularly concerning this *Mystery* of the *Trinity*. It ought then to satisfy us that there is sufficient evidence that this Doctrine is delivered in *Scripture*, and that what is there declared concerning it doth not imply a Contradiction."[36] If Scripture contains "mysteries"—something above, though not contradictory to, reason—we must hold fast to it. We cannot pick and choose among the truths of Scripture, appropriating to ourselves only those with which reason in a narrow sense feels comfortable. Reasonable or not, truths in Scripture, because they are there, must be believed.

Granted the integrity of Scripture in this sense, what helps does one have in establishing whether an individual text is Trinitarian? Of the major divines, Tillotson had the most bias against any but the earliest Fathers of the Church and their interpretations of texts. Intending to convince Socinians of their error, he did not use authorities to do so whom the Socinians held responsible for the mysteries of the Trinity in the first place. But Tillotson would not allow that "the most ancient writers of the Christian Church" and "the sense of all *Antiquity*" were anti-Trinitarian. Tillotson also used the scriptural context as an aid to the interpretation of problem texts, understanding the first chapter of the Gospel of John, for example, in the light of the Wisdom literature of the Old Testament. Classical authors such as Plutarch may also be useful to understand the Greek usage of the Pauline epistles. In regard to external helps, Tillotson speaks of a "general Tradition" of the church as to the meaning of Trinitarian texts, but he is careful not to situate this tradition so clearly in the clergy, as South does. The first of the 1679–80 sermons insists that the interpreter be aware of historical context. Socinus had interpreted the phrase of St. John, "In the beginning was the Word," as referring to the time when the Gospel began to be preached. Tillotson counters that John's prologue cannot only be interpreted by "Reason and Wit . . . without understanding the Historical occasion of it."[37] In his contextual study, Tillotson shows that John's phraseology was a compromise between the proto-Arianism of early heretics and the extended mystical language of the gnostics. Reference to the latter is especially important because Tillotson wants to show that John, like the Socinians and himself, reacts to overconceptualization of the Gospel, but, unlike the Socinians, remains a believer in the divinity of Jesus.

A survey of Tillotson's contributions to the Socinian debates of the 1690s illustrates the difficulty of trying to respond to the tracts by using the traditional methods of scriptural interpretation which the divines had been practicing since the early 1660s. Tillotson perfectly illustrates the dilemma pointed out by Richard Simon; Tillotson and the Socinians claim to rely on the same principles—the literal sense, the early Fathers, and common sense—and reach opposing conclusions as to what Scripture says. Tillotson charges that Socinian scriptural interpretation is novel and "violent," a term he frequently uses. He charges that Socinus himself avoided the literal sense "by Criticizing upon words, and searching into all the senses that they are possibly capable of, till he can find one, though never so forc'd and foreign, that will save harmless the Opinion, which he was before hand resolved to maintain even against the most natural and obvious sense of the Text."[38] But Socinians also bring this charge of pre-scriptural bias against Trinitarian theologians; both sides claim that only they are reading the Scripture literally, with the subsidiary help of the most ancient authors of the church.

Tillotson only glances at one possible way out of this impasse—the way of textual criticism, allegedly based on an impartial survey of the extant ancient copies. He asserts that 1 John 5:7 ("For there are three that bear record in heaven, the Father, the Word, and the Holy Ghost: and these three are one"), a debated text, may be found, in its Trinitarian form, in most ancient copies. But Tillotson uses 1 Timothy 3:16 ("God was manifest in the flesh"), which the Socinians claim as non-Trinitarian, as if there were no debate about its Trinitarian reference.[39] In the interim between the delivery (1679–80) and publication (1693) of his four sermons, did Tillotson become aware of the implications of Richard Simon's *Critical History*, translated in 1682? There is no evidence that he did become aware of Simon's work. Like others of his contemporaries discussed in the last chapter, Tillotson presumably thought Brian Walton's textual work had said the last word; a proper text established, the bases of doctrine were clear.

Stillingfleet made a more extensive and penetrating critique of the Socinian tracts than any of his contemporaries. Like Tillotson, Stillingfleet republished an earlier work during the controversy, a tract on the satisfaction for sin paid by Christ, published first in 1669 and again in 1696. Likewise, Stillingfleet composed new anti-Socinian material: two sermons, "The Mysteries of the Christian Faith Asserted and Vindicated" (April 7, 1691) and a Christmas sermon of 1693; and a heavily argued tract, *A Discourse in Vindication of the Trinity* (1696). A second essay on the sacrificial role of Christ, written sometime in the 1690s, was published posthumously. Stillingfleet's major accomplishment was twofold: he enunciated with precision and power the divines' position on mystery and on literal interpretation, and he fully integrated the new textual criticism into a Trinitarian theology.

Commenting on the nature of Jesus' redemptive action, Stillingfleet writes, in brief, a sublime essay on the traditional relationship of Scripture to doctrine:

There is a great Difficulty as to the Way of *saving sinners* by *Christ Jesus*; whether by *the Doctrine and Example of the Man Christ Jesus, by the Power he attained through his Sufferings*; Or, *by the Eternal Son of God's assuming our Nature, and suffering in our stead in order to the reconciling God to us and making a Propitiation for our Sins.* These are two very different *Hypotheses* or Notions of *Christ's coming to save sinners*; and the former seems more easie to be understood and believed; and the other seems to have insuperable Difficulties in point of Reason; and to run our Religion into *Mysteries*, which expose our Faith and make Christianity appear contemptible to Men of Sense and Understanding. . . .

These are plausible Insinuations, and would be apt to prevail on considering Men's minds, if they were to form and make a Religion that might be most accommodated to the *Genius* and *Humour* of the Age they live in. And truly no Men (by their own Authority) can pretend to a Right to impose on others any *Mysteries of Faith*, or any such things which are above their Capacity to understand. But that is not our Case; for we all profess to believe and receive *Christianity* as a *Divine Revelation*; and God (we say) may require from us the belief of what we may not be able to comprehend, especially if it relates to himself, or such things which are consequent upon the Union of the Divine and Humane Nature. Therefore our business is to consider, whether any such things be contained in that *Revelation* which we all own; and if they be, we are bound to believe them, although we are not able to comprehend them.[40]

The criticisms of the Socinians against priestcraft and a lifelong habit of trying to make theology plain and clear have had their impact: one must be reluctant to admit the category "mystery" into Christian theology. Stillingfleet nevertheless insists, like Tillotson, that the entire content of Scripture must be accounted for. If the scriptural data resist understanding, no matter what the genius of the age toward rationalization, Scripture must be put before the complaints of an aggrieved intellect. The term "common-sense" philosophy and theology has in recent years been applied to Stillingfleet and his peers. It is a useful term to understand his arguments, which frequently appeal to the common sense of his hearers and readers. But it does not prepare us for his argument in a key passage such as this, in which common sense is honored, then rejected, as the final norm for establishing the contents of revelation.

When two meanings of a passage conflict, how does one choose between them? Stillingfleet summarizes the divines' position:

Now according to reason we may judge that Sense to be preferr'd.

(1.) Which is most plain and easie and agreeable to the most received Sense of Words; not that which is forced and intricate, or which puts improper and *metaphorical* Senses upon Words which are commonly taken in other Senses; especially when it is no Sacramental thing, which in its own Nature is Figurative.

(2.) That which suits most with the Scope and Design not only of the particular Places, but of the whole *New Testament*; which is, to magnifie God and to depress Man; to set forth, the infinite Love and Condescention of God *in giving his Son to be a Propitiation for our Sins*; to set up the Worship of one *true God* in Opposition to *Creatures*; to represent and declare the mighty Advantages Mankind receive by the *Sufferings* of *Christ Jesus*.

(3.) That which hath been generally received in the *Christian Church* to be the Sense of those places. For, we are certain, this was always look'd on as a matter of great Concernment to all Christians; and they had as great Capacity of understanding the Sense of the Apostles; and the Primitive Church had greater helps for knowing it than others at so much greater Distance. And therefore the Sense is not to be taken from modern *Inventions* or *Criticisms*, or Pretences to *Revelation*; but that which was as first deliver'd to the *Christian Church* and hath been since received and embraced by it in the several Ages; and hath been most strenuously asserted, when it hath met with Opposition, as founded on *Scripture* and the *general Consent* of the *Christian Church*.

(4.) That which best agrees with the *Characters* of those Persons from whom we receive the Christian Faith; and those are *Christ Jesus* and his *holy Apostles*. For, if their *Authority* be lost, our Religion is gone; and their Authority depends upon their *Sincerity* and *Faithfulness*, and Care to inform the World aright in matters of so great Importance.[41]

Elsewhere, as in his first point, Stillingfleet warns against looking in Scripture for metaphor where none is intended: he says that the verbal paucity, idiom, and naturally concrete nature of biblical Hebrew make it perilous to indulge oneself in "all possible significations."[42] One must have a feeling for the nature of the medium of communication. Stillingfleet does not actually contrast the abstraction of a modern philosophical mind with the more imagistic Hebrew intelligence, but that seems to be his point. It is interesting to see both Stillingfleet and Tillotson moving away, in the Socinian debates, from the unquestioned preference for generalization that marks much late seventeenth-century commentary, especially evident in its discussions of inspiration. Committed to the wholeness of Scripture, they suggest that parts of the wholeness must be taken on their own terms, which resist abstraction.

Stillingfleet says, in his second point, that the scope and design of Scripture partly aim "to depress Man"; like Tillotson, he objects to carrying preconceived human constructs to Scripture and imposing them on it. He writes elsewhere: "The main strength of our Adversaries is not pretended to lie in the Scriptures; all the care they have of them is only to reconcile them if possible with their *Hypothesis*." He characterizes Socinian interpretation as posing not only a methodological problem but also a moral one; it involves a human stance of pride which all the Scriptures speak against. Such pride is also evident when interpretation disagrees with, in his third point, "the *general Consent* of the *Christian Church*." Stillingfleet undergirds his attack on the violence of Socinian interpretation with an extensive summary of the early Fathers of the Church on the question of the Trinity. By referring, in his fourth point, to the character of Jesus and the apostles, Stillingfleet means that the interpretation of passages concerning Jesus' divinity must take into account the humility of Jesus and the plain speaking of the apostles. The Scriptures show that neither makes unfounded claims to preeminence. If such claims are in Scripture, their truth is reinforced by the honest characters of the claimants.[43] The argument involves the standard apologetics for the divine authority of Scripture and is perhaps more useful in that context.

Although Stillingfleet fully responded to the imagistic quality of scriptural language, he did not back away from involved, abstract argument about traditional ways in which theology had tried to restate scriptural truth. Stillingfleet's best-known work is his controversy with Locke on substance, which began in the last chapter of his 1696 *Vindication of the Trinity* and continued in his two responses to Locke's letters.[44] The ability to analyze abstract concepts also marks his directly anti-Socinian material. In a sustained way, for example, he attempts to show how a mystery like the Trinity does not contradict reason; he freely enters into debate on the nature of such abstract concepts as the nature of inherited guilt and of a sufficient cause for divine punishment.[45] Although South and Tillotson showed interest in such abstract argument, Stillingfleet seems to have had the most relish for answering those Socinian tracts which deal less with the interpretation of primary texts and more with subsequent theological formulations.

Stillingfleet first encountered Simonian higher criticism in his sermon of February 1682/3, which he never published. By 1696, in the *Vindication*, he had begun to assimilate the new textual scholarship into his own scriptural interpretations. In chapter 8 of that work, "The Socinian Sense of Scripture Examined," he argues on critical grounds—on the evidence of extant, early copies of Scripture—that the Trinitarian interpretation of key Pauline texts, such as 1 Timothy 3:16, is founded on critical readings of the best copies; Stillingfleet alludes to Simon, by name, in support of his position.[46] Stillingfleet turns the tables on the Socinians and even Simon himself, who cast doubt on the possibility that even the critical point of view could resolve the Socinian controversy. This occurred at the end of Stillingfleet's life, in one of his very last theological works. At the very end of the time charted for this present study, we find Anglican scriptural interpretation, at least as expressed by one prominent divine, supple enough to bend to and align itself with the new techniques for reading a text.

One may now examine how Anglican scriptural interpretation changed under the brunt of Socinian critique. That it did change is clear in at least two instances. First, the divines still maintained, in the 1690s, that saving truths are clear and plain in the literal sense of Scripture and that these saving truths include the Trinity, Incarnation, and real satisfaction made by Jesus; yet the methodology of South, Tillotson, and Stillingfleet had clearly backed away from the position that the simplest reader may perceive these truths without special help. South's advocacy of a privileged order of interpreters, Tillotson's demand for a contextual reading, and Stillingfleet's forays into scholastic disputation and textual criticism all speak the same admission: in an atmosphere of increasing rationalist pressure, it is no longer possible to maintain that any person may simply pick up Scripture and find therein its saving truths. At the very least, a university education would seem a prerequisite for finding out what Scripture says about the Trinity and Incarnation. Stillingfleet and Tillotson, oriented more than South toward a broader church, avoided suggesting that a privileged central authority must interpret Scripture; yet their methodologies imply the necessity for a learned cadre of established interpreters.

The idea that specialists are needed for a full interpretation of Scripture is not new to Anglican scriptural interpretation in the seventeenth century; what is new is that such a cadre of specialists may be necessary to determine the saving truths of Scripture, among which prominently stand the Trinity, the divinity of Jesus, and Jesus' precise role in the economy of salvation. Tillotson did not seem to be fully aware of the discrepancies between his own method of scholarly interpretation and his habitual thesis that all literate readers may easily find the saving truths of Scripture. In his anti-Socinian writing, he twice reasserts that thesis.[47] Yet few common readers could have had the learning to initiate his recovery of historical context; surely few readers, besides the learned divines, had the knowledge of gnosticism and of first-century heresies at hand that Tillotson says is necessary to understand the literal meaning of the first chapter of John's Gospel.

Second, the fuller development of the concept of mystery in the 1690s deemphasized the divines' previous insistence on the clarity and distinctness of scriptural doctrine. One finds without difficulty the admission of the category of mystery in the divines writing before the 1690s. The Socinians forced the divines to bring this category to the forefront of their theological project. As the divines did so, the "reasonableness" of the core doctrines of Christianity seemed to fade. A greater discrepancy appears between the alleged clarity of scriptural revelation and what in fact is not clear and distinct—its very essence. To the thesis that Scripture is Socinian, the divines answered that even the earliest Christian writers claimed it to be Trinitarian; Stillingfleet added the important critical observation that the best copies of Scripture also enunciate Trinitarian doctrine. To the Socinians' insistence that the doctrine of the Trinity contradicts reason, the divines responded that the doctrine is above and not against reason and as to the clear manner of its existence, reason itself can have nothing infallible to say.

IV

The relationships of Tillotson and John Locke with Socinianism run, to a certain extent, along parallel lines. Like Tillotson, Locke was accused of being a Socinian and, during the 1690s, wrote extensively to deny the charge.[48] That both Tillotson and especially Locke advocated toleration, a Socinian cause also, did nothing to separate them, in the minds of some, from the stigma of subtle Socinian advocacy. Even twentieth-century historians such as Herbert McLachlan and Maurice Cranston stress Locke's Socinian or Unitarian views.[49] Unlike Tillotson, however, Locke never took the simplest self-defense against such charges: an explicit espousal of Trinitarian doctrine. A number of reasons can be made out why Locke did not do this, including the possibility that he did not believe that the doctrine of the Trinity, as it was taught by seventeenth-century Anglicans, was clearly expressed by Scripture.[50] When charged with denying orthodox doctrine, Locke habitually defended himself not by affirming the doctrine but by denying that he denied it. It is clear from all of Locke's writing about Scripture that he thought that far more doctrines were being proved from Scripture than Scripture expressly taught. He did not want to add to the sum of scriptural doctrine; he especially did not want to add or spell out controversial doctrine that could, in the hands of the magistrate, be used to force theological uniformity.

It is in fact wrongheaded to approach Locke's writings on Scripture from the point of view of doctrine. All the evidence shows that Locke strenuously avoided the label of any party. Again and again he attacked those who sought to superimpose preconceived doctrine on Scripture. Among the "systems" of doctrines he accused of this, he included the Socinian:

The same genius seems to influence them all, even those who pretend most to freedom, the Socinians themselves. For when it is observed, how positive and eager they are in their disputes; how forward they are to have their interpretations of Scripture received for authentic, though to others, in several places, they seem very much strained; how impatient they are of contradiction; and with what disrespect and roughness they often treat their opposers: may it not be suspected, that this so visible a warmth in their present circumstances, and zeal for their orthodoxy, would (had they the power) work in them as it does in others?[51]

The interpreter who imposes doctrine on Scripture does violence to the scriptural text: this interpretive situation is, for Locke, a microcosm of the situation wherein a magistrate imposes a religion on the state against its will.

Locke writes somewhat more ambiguously about the possibility of mystery in Scripture. In *An Essay Concerning Human Understanding* (1690), he clearly distinguishes things "above reason" from things "contrary to reason," using the resurrection of the dead as an example of a truth above reason.[52] It was never part of Locke's theological project to show that all religious truth must be presented to the mind in clear and distinct ideas and that what cannot be cast in such cannot be required for belief. When Locke speaks of mystery, he does not reject it outright, as do the Socinian tracts; he nevertheless sometimes treats it as if it were not a permanent category of scriptural thought but something Jesus and the Spirit had finally cleared up.[53] The Socinian tracts occasionally speak this way.

What is Locke's method for reading Scripture? He is, first, a severe and simple inductionist. One prepares oneself to find the meaning of Scripture by rigorously wiping away all preconceptions; even the chapter and verse divisions of the Pauline epistles become blinders to the full meaning of an individual letter, which must be read, as a whole, at one sitting.[54] The Fathers of the Church are ignored, although Locke occasionally uses seventeenth-century Anglican theologians such as Chillingworth and Tillotson to support his own readings.[55] Some reference must be made to meanings of scriptural words "such as they may be supposed to have had in the mouths of the speakers, who used them according to the language of that time and country wherein they lived,"[56] although Locke does not develop this principle of interpretation. The great teachers of what Scripture says are Christ himself and the Spirit: "I know of no other infallible guide, but the Spirit of God in the Scriptures."[57]

Led by the Spirit, brushing aside all previous commentary and theological doctrine, the inductive reader finds in Scripture what must be believed, what is indubitably its content. "Nor perhaps do those wander very far from the truth who are of the opinion," Locke wrote to van Limborch in 1694, "that nothing should be imposed upon the consciences of Christians except what is contained in the clear and express words of Holy Writ."[58] In the four Gospels and Acts, Locke finds in the clearest terms what all Christians must believe to call themselves by that name: that Jesus is the Messiah. *The Reasonableness of Christianity* (1695) is devoted, in an analysis of text after text, to showing this truth: "All that was to be believed for justification, was no more but this single proposition that 'Jesus of Nazareth was the Christ, or the Messiah.'"[59]

Locke understood that Scripture teaches other doctrines than that Jesus is the Messiah. Like Chillingworth, he refused to make a list of fundamental doctrines; in argument with John Edwards, a critic of the 1695 work, he insisted on the danger and practical impossibility of doing so. Locke disliked the distinction between necessary and unnecessary matters in Scripture, for "all that is contained in the inspired writings is all of divine authority, must be allowed for such, and received for divine and infallible truth by every subject of Christ's Kingdom, i.e., Christian." In Locke's writings we may still perceive a hierarchy among these unnamed doctrines. On the first level of the New Testament is the doctrine that Jesus is the Messiah. Belief in this doctrine specifically makes a person a

Christian; this is what is absolutely required because it is indubitably taught. Locke further distinguishes other levels of scriptural truths: "very plain," easily understood propositions, which demand "explicit belief," and others of more difficulty and ambiguity, which require the help of the Spirit to understand;[60] propositions that are in the express words of Scripture and others that are deduced from them;[61] propositions whose belief is necessary to salvation and others necessary only to belong to a specific communion;[62] propositions promulgated at the start of Christianity and those promulgated later.[63] It is left to the reader to assign an individual doctrine taught by Scripture or deduced from Scripture to one or other of these categories. Locke's strong views on toleration again motivated his refusal to create a hierarchy of named doctrines. Much of his studied coyness in this area is accounted for by his insistence that no writings of his own ever be allowed to justify a creed to be forced on believers.

We know from Locke's notebooks and extant correspondence that he was familiar with the critical work of Richard Simon.[64] Yet textual criticism seems, at first, to play no part in Locke's determination to find essential doctrine in the Gospels and Acts. Locke's published works avoid the arguments over textual readings that mark the Socinian tracts and Stillingfleet's *Vindication*. Nevertheless, we may surmise that Locke had Simonian criticism very much in mind in *The Reasonableness of Christianity*. Therein he tries to argue a conclusion with which no one who knows the involved books can possibly disagree. No textual criticism can seriously detract from the mass of texts and the inductive conclusion that Jesus said he was the Messiah and demanded belief in this for membership in his kingdom. Simon had said that Scripture alone cannot resolve the Trinitarian controversy. Locke lets this pass and searches to find only unassailable doctrine. While insisting on the *sola Scriptura*, he uses this principle to isolate only unassailable ground. We may infer that, partly because of textual problems, Locke considers the Trinity to be an ambiguous scriptural doctrine or one imposed on Scripture; we may infer that Locke had internalized Simonian criticism in this regard. But Locke himself is publicly silent on this point, and it is indeed a point on which his writings offer maximum resistance to certifying our inferences concerning his personal beliefs.

Locke agreed with the major Anglican divines of his day that faith primarily assents to propositions, not to a person.[65] Recent commentary has contributed much to the discussion of the concept of faith in Locke;[66] unlike the divines, Locke does not use the term "knowledge" in regard to faith. But this stance is not taken to minimize the importance of faith, as in Spinoza; rather, we have "knowledge" of very little and it is faith which gives meaning to life. "We have certain knowledge of our own existence, of God's existence, of mathematical propositions, and very little else," writes Richard Ashcraft of Locke's thought as a whole. "Beyond that narrow island of certainty extends the great ocean of probability, whose waters we may expect at any time to see parted by a revelation from God."[67]

In the discussion of reason and faith in chapter 18 of book 4 of *An Essay Concerning Human Understanding*, context is an important factor. At the end of chapter 17, Locke says he will address those who separate reason and faith; chapter 19, from the fourth edition on, contains a criticism of "*Enthusiasm*. Which laying by Reason would set up Revelation without it." Such a context suggests that Locke wants to prove not the irrationality of faith in chapter 18 but, granted that it is not knowledge, to show what about it is rational—against any who would suggest that faith consists in some private revelation that reason cannot judge. In this, then, Locke's task, given a change in terms, resembles that of the major divines of his time: "To all those who pretend not to immediate *Revelation*, but are required to pay Obedience, and to receive the Truths revealed to others, which, by the Tradition of Writings, or Word of Mouth, are conveyed down to them, Reason has a great deal more to do, and is that only which can induce us to receive them."[68]

Locke's controversy of 1696 and 1697 with Bishop Stillingfleet casts helpful light on this matter. Stillingfleet maintained that Locke's philosophical formulations of substance and personal identity provide inadequate or hostile concepts in which to address the scriptural doctrines of the Trinity and the resurrection of the dead.[69] Locke argues in response first that such doctrines, as Stillingfleet formulates them, are deductions from Scripture, not Scripture itself. "I do not here question their truth," he writes, "nor deny that they may be drawn from Scripture: but I deny that these very propositions [concerning natures and persons] are in express words in my Bible." Second, Locke turns the tables on the bishop, arguing that we should not attempt to prove the internal rationality of revealed doctrine, as if "divine revelation abates of its credibility in all those articles it proposes, proportionable as human reason fails to support the testimony of God."[70] Even though Locke here rejects attempts to prove the reasonableness of Scripture on internal evidence, we should not overly stress the differences between the positions of the adversaries. Locke affirms in the *Essay* that some truths in Scripture may also be found by reason alone.[71] It is apparently only Stillingfleet's attempt to show how the Trinity, for example, does not contradict reason that bothers Locke and leads him to suggest that the bishop has set up norms by which some propositions in or about Scripture may be preferred to others on the grounds of internal probability.

How, then, does Locke relate reason to Scripture? He seems principally to rely on the argument from testimony. Faith is assent on the grounds of the speaker's credibility; it is reason's task to show that an individual doctrine in Scripture is divine testimony. To accomplish this, Locke relies on the doctrine of miracles that had been fully developed by Stillingfleet and others: "It is plain, that where the miracle is admitted, the doctrine cannot be rejected; it comes with the assurance of a divine attestation to him that allows the miracle, and he cannot question its truth."[72] By suppressing internal rational evidence and heightening the external evidence of testimony, Locke, the lay philosopher of the Enlightenment, suggests that Stillingfleet, the episcopal defender of Anglican orthodoxy, is a rationalist! But taken as a whole, with their corresponding emphases on the argument from testimony, the teachings of the divines and of Locke on the truth of Scripture scarcely conflict.

What, then, are we to make of the title of Locke's most sustained theological work, *The Reasonableness of Christianity*? A few months before it appeared in print, Locke wrote of its origins to van Limborch:

For this winter, considering diligently wherein the Christian faith consists, I thought that it ought to be drawn from the very fountains of Holy Writ, the opinions and orthodoxies of sects and systems, whatever they may be, being set aside. From an intent and careful reading of the New Testament the conditions of the New Covenant and the teaching of the Gospel became clearer to me, as it seemed to me, than the noontide light, and I am fully convinced that a sincere reader of the Gospel cannot be in doubt as to what the Christian faith is.[73]

In the "Second Vindication," Locke writes that the work is also written "for those who were not fully satisfied of the reasonableness" of Christianity and that "my book was chiefly designed for Deists."[74] I do not know that we can fully reconcile these different accounts of the genesis of *The Reasonableness of Christianity*. From internal evidence, one gathers that the "reasonableness" of Christianity meant for Locke, in 1695, what is plainly, simply, and incontrovertibly taught by the four Gospels and Acts, the principal historical sections of the New Testament. "Reasonableness" thus means the *ratio* or essence of the object in view, unencumbered by the presuppositions sectarian commentators bring to it. It is difficult to see how Deists, who presumably would expect some discussion of the internal reasonableness of Scripture or of Christian doctrine, would find the work, as it is, very convincing.

An attempt to understand Locke's title brings us again to what has been a principal theme of the preceding study of Anglican scriptural interpretation in the later seventeenth century: that when seventeenth-century Anglicans such as Stillingfleet, Tillotson, and Locke used the words "reason" and "reasonableness" in regard to Scripture, the terms must be interpreted in a broad sense. Only in the case of a few doctrines such as the existence of God and the immortality of the soul do these authors consider that natural reason can and should fully prove that the individual contents of Scripture are fully true. By the "reasonableness of Christianity" these authors primarily meant that Scripture can reasonably be shown to come from God, through the argument from testimony, and that, befitting its source, the saving truth of Scripture has a decorous simplicity and plainness.

Conclusion

MANY Anglicans after 1700 found the synthesis of scriptural revelation and human reason by the divines of the late seventeenth century of lasting importance. Although the theological curriculum of the eighteenth-century university is difficult to reconstruct, it appears that especially the sermons of Archbishop Tillotson were a staple of clerical education and a source of ideas before and after ordination. In the first half of the century and later, the rise of the novel also testifies to the popularity of the divines' sermons among lay and clerical readers. In Samuel Richardson's *Clarissa* (1747–48), for example, the heroine thinks more highly of her captors when she finds volumes of South's and Tillotson's sermons in their house.[1] Laurence Sterne's *Tristram Shandy* (1760–67) shows awareness of Tillotson's thought; Sterne's own published sermons extensively borrow from the archbishop's.[2] Tillotson's collected sermons (1695–1704), in fourteen volumes arranged around different themes, became a *summa theologica anglicana* for succeeding generations. The many editions of the sermons in the first half of the century testify, as L. P. Curtis writes, to "their enormous influence" as theological and moral guides.[3]

The influence of the divines lasted well into the nineteenth century. In his *Apologia Pro Vita Sua* (1864), John Henry Newman writes of his struggles with seventeenth-century divinity before his conversion from the Church of England to Roman Catholicism in 1845. The confident theologizing of Barrow, Stillingfleet, and others had, Newman felt, misled him; his conscience demanded, however, that he encounter their arguments once again before he left the church of his birth, a church whose identity and strength the divines had definitively articulated.[4]

Without a doubt the insistent presence of the divines' thought for a century and a half is owing to their repeated demonstrations that the whole of Scripture and the troubling demands of human reason were compatible, and that no argument brought forward by secular philosophy and scholarship could alter that compatibility. As I have shown, the divines' concept of reason and their scholarship were not as finely honed as those of Spinoza, Toland, Simon, and others. From the point of view of the history of philosophy, the attenuated rationalism of the divines may be perceived as a deficiency. From the point of view of the educated lay person or cleric of succeeding generations, however, the divines' stance must have seemed compelling: confident but not claiming too much, massive in scope but descending sufficiently into detail to suggest that all contrary evidence had been considered. Even today the argumentative energy and learning of the divines are impressive. Their project gave comfort to average believers who could afford the purchase of Tillotson's sermons, but not the time and energy to evaluate their every argument. Surely Newman's agony over the divines' apologetics was the exception rather than the rule.

Today readers of eighteenth-century sermons find an emphasis on morality and virtue to be their dominant characteristic. This moralistic strain owes a great deal to the influence of the divines. Barrow, South, Stillingfleet, and Tillotson very often preached about Judaeo-Christian morality, as well as about the dogmatic issues I have stressed in this study. Morality forms one strong basis of any lifetime of preaching, and the divines were not anomalous in this respect. In a deeper sense, because of their encounters with heterodox thought, the divines freed later preachers from absorption in dogmatic concerns. It was a common idea in the eighteenth century, an idea also fostered by the divines, that squabbling over theological issues was scandalous; the limited energies of the preacher had best be expended in urging believers to a life of virtue based on a few unassailable truths in Scripture. A confidence in the clear establishment of those truths was the gift of late seventeenth-century Anglican divines to their church.

Appendix I

Stillingfleet Responds to Simon and Spinoza: Ms. 0.81, St. John's College, Cambridge

BOUND Ms. 0.81 was given to St. John's College, Cambridge, in 1895 by its then senior bursar, Robert Forsyth Scott, who later served as master from 1908 to 1933. The college library Donations Book (1892–1904) lists Scott's gift for January 18, 1895: "Stillingfleet (Ed.) Bp. Sermons in MS. of Bp. Stillingfleet, four of which have not been printed." Apart from a verbatim repetition of this entry in the college magazine, the *Eagle* (18 [1895]: 629), there do not seem to be any other printed college records of the gift at the time.

On the flyleaf verso is written, "This Book is Bp. Stillingfleet's Handwriting" and "The Sermons in short hand I cannot decypher: the other four are *not* included among the printed Sermons of Bishop Stillingfleet. Edw Wm Stillingfleet." The writer is apparently Edward William Stillingfleet (1782–1866), a descendant of the bishop and a fellow of Lincoln College, Oxford, from 1812 to 1833 (*Alumni Oxonienses*, ed. Joseph Foster [1888], 4:1355). Where the manuscript rested after E. W. Stillingfleet's death and where R. F. Scott found it are not known.

The first one hundred leaves of the bound manuscript are numbered on the recto side and contain four sermons, which, as E. W. Stillingfleet writes, are not published elsewhere:

(1) Fols. 1–24. A sermon on Jeremiah 17:19, given on December 11, 1682, at "Mercers Chappel."

(2) Fols. 25–49. A sermon on Luke 19:31, given on February 23, 1682/3, at Whitehall.

(3) Fols. 50–74. A sermon on 1 Timothy 3:5, given on April 4, 1683, at "St. Clements," "Lent Sermon."

(4) Fols. 75–100. A sermon on John 20:29, given on "Easter Day" 1683 at Whitehall.

About fifteen more leaves are bound in the book; these are written in the shorthand E. W. Stillingfleet complains that he cannot "decypher."

Because the second sermon entails Bishop Stillingfleet's responses to Richard Simon's *L'histoire critique du Vieux Testament* (1678) and Spinoza's *Tractatus Theologico-Politicus* (1670), the sermon is of importance for the history of scriptural interpretation in late seventeenth-century England. I have here transcribed the section of the sermon dealing with these two works. I have expanded Stillingfleet's many superscripted contractions but have otherwise attempted to leave his spelling and punctuation as they are in MS. 0.81. When I have not been able to understand the bishop's hand, I indicate omissions by ellipses. I have included most of his marginal notes in the text, in brackets.

When Stillingfleet quotes from Spinoza and Simon, his translations and summaries are sometimes only loosely based on the text, and his page references are, as often as not, inexact. Stillingfleet's own copies of Spinoza and Simon may be examined at Marsh's Library, Dublin. He owned a 1670 edition of Spinoza's *Tractatus* (Marsh P.1.4.48) and two copies of Simon's *L'histoire critique*, a French edition of 1680 (Marsh B.2.3.26) and an English translation of 1682 (Marsh B.2.2.42). It was not Stillingfleet's custom to annotate his books, and the three texts provide only the following exception to the rule: on the title page of the anonymous *Tractatus* of 1670 is written, in what seems to be Stillingfleet's hand, "Spinoza (Bened.)."

I am grateful to Joel H. Fishman for informing me of the existence of manuscript 0.81, to A. G. Lee, librarian of St. John's College, for his personal assistance, and to the master and fellows of St. John's College, Cambridge, for permission to print the following.

/30ʳ/ I shall endeavor to shew, 1. That the Writings of Moses are genuine & sincere. 2. That the Prophets spake not from the heat of Imagination, but from Divine Inspiration. 3. That what is contained in their writings is sufficient to perswade Men to Repent. 1. That the Writings of Moses are genuine & sincere. The Question is not, whether the Books of Moses were written by himself, or by others according to his Appointment or Direction. It is not, whether the Writings of Moses were preserved free from all literal mistakes, or varieties of Readings in matters of no great consequence. It is not, whether upon the Review after the Captivity, some names of Places /30ᵛ/ might be changed, & some few additional passages injected to compleat the History, & to give an account of the death of the Persons at the end of their Books, while there were yet Prophets among them. /31ʳ/ Whether these things be true or false they do not come under our present debate. But it is a Question of great weight & moment, & whereon very much depends, whether the Books of Moses contain the genuine Writings or onely some Abstracts & Abridgements of them, full of interpolations, repetitions, transpositions, etc. /30ᵛ/ as is pretended by a late Writer in great vogue among those who are glad to find any thing that seems to reflect on the Authority of the Scriptures; as in Truth this supposition doth too much [*Histoire critique du Vieux Testament*, I. 5–77]. /31ʳ/ For then the Certainty of our Faith doth not depend on the Authority of Moses or the Prophets, but on the Credibility of those Persons, who have taken upon them to give out these Abridgements in stead of their Original Writings. And how can any man be secure that something very material is not left out, as it often happens in the making Abridgements; or that something is not inserted contrary to the meaning of the Original? Where both are at hand to compare, every one may judge; but to suppose the true Originals lost & onely some imperfect Rhapsodies left us is to reflect as much on the Authority of the Scriptures, as men can do without denying it. It is a vain thing to pretend *to acknowledge the Providence of God in the preservation of the Book of Scripture, which hath passed through so many Hands & Ages* [I. 1], when at the same time it is asserted that the Original Books are lost, & onely some confused Copies remain; which seems to be rather /32ʳ/ a deceiving than owning Providence: as if a Man should pretend to admire the Providence of God in preserving the Words of Trogus or Dio, & at the same time should declare that we have nothing entire of them left, having onely the Contractions of Justin & Xiphiline, & those very much corrupted too. Neither is it any better Salvation for the Authority of the Books of Scripture to pretend *that these Copies were given out to the People by a sort of Prophets who made the Additions*

& Alterations by the direction of the Spirit of God [Preface, p. 3; I.1]. For what Divine Assistance could those then have, who were guilty of so many faults in their own Copies? For either the charge against the present Copies is true, or false; if it is true, as is pretended, what blasphemy is it to charge so much disorder & Confusion, so many interpolations & repetitions on the Holy Spirit of God? Besides, what assurance can we have of any thing like Divine Inspiration in these Publick Writers who preserved the Originals in the Sacred Registeries & gave out imperfect Copies? We read of no miracles they wrought, no Prophecies of theirs accomplished, no Testimony given to them by the other Prophets; how then should we come to believing them true Prophets? or so much as men of common fidelity who would dare to bring such a dishonour on the Sacred Books, as to give out corrupt & confused transcripts of them, when they had the pure Originals in their Custody? /33ʳ/ Having said this much to shew the bad Consequences of this Opinion, I now come to shew the falseness of it. And that I shall do by these 2 things. 1. That all the Arguments that are now urged against the genuineness of the Books of Moses would equally have held in the time of Christ & his Apostles. 2. That not withstanding, Christ & his Apostles do sufficiently vindicate & assert the Authority of them. 1. That all the Arguments now used against the genuineness of the Books would have equally held in the Time of Christ & his Apostles, for no other corruptions, or transpositions, or interpolations are so much as pretended but what were before our Saviours time: If any disorder happen'd by the misplacing of the several little scrolls upon the Roller, which was the ancient way of making up their Volume, this must have been done before the Synagogue Way of Worship was set up; for after that, the Books of Moses & the Prophets were so constantly read & the Law so well known among the Jews [Acts 15:21], that it were a thing impossible to sophisticate the Copies without being taken notice of. But much more impossible for the Jews to do it since the Books of Moses have been so universally received among the Christians & such perpetual disputes between them & the Jews about the sense & meaning of them. If there were any such Prophets who had Power to review, to correct & alter the former Books, they must be while the Jewish Commonwealth flourished, & not long after the return /34ʳ/ from Captivity; but whether the present Collection of sacred Books was made soon or sometime after, is not material

to us, as long as it is acknowledged to have been received as it is, before the time of Christ & his Apostles. 2. That notwithstanding these suppositions, they do sufficiently assert & vindicate the Authority of the Books of Moses. For is it reasonable to suppose that our Bl. Saviour, who shewd so much zeal in vindicating the Law against the false Glosses & interpretations of the Scribes & Pharisees, should not let fall one word implying any corruption or interpolation of the text of the Law itself? But on the contrary he saith, that *till Heaven & Earth passe, one jote or Tittle shall not passe from the Law till all be fulfilled* [Matthew 5:18]. How could our Saviour speak this, if he knew of many alterations that had been made in the Body of the Law after the time of Moses? For although it be sometime pretended that the alterations were only in the Historical passages; yet elsewhere it is said *that they were in the very Laws & Ordinances themselves* [I.5. p. 32]. Would our Lord & Saviour declare so much of the perpetual nature of that Law without any Connotation, if he knew any part of it not to be genuine & sincere? Why our Saviour expressly calls them the *Writings of Moses* & appeals to them as such in the disputes between him & the Jews. *For had ye believed Moses*, saith he, *ye would have believed me: for he wrote of me. But if ye believe not his Writings, how shall ye believe my Words* [John 5:46]? Can anything be plainer than that our Saviour doth attribute /35ʳ/ the Books then extant to Moses & takes it for granted that they were his genuine Writings? If there had been any corruptions or interpolations at the time in them the arguments had been fallacious for they had not been the true Writings of Moses, but onely such as had born his Name. But our Saviour urges the Jews with the Authority & Testimony of Moses, *there is one that accuseth them, even Moses in whom ye trust* [45]. And then he proves this from the Authentick Writings which were of no force, if there had been any ground to suspect any alterations that had been made in his Writings by other hands. When the Question happend with the Pharisees about Divorce, our Saviour reduces the point to the first Institution of Marriage, & repeats it out of the History of Creation in the very Words of Moses [Matthew 19:4–5; Genesis 1:27, 2:24]. If this were such a confused, disorderly narration of things as is pretended [*Hist. Crit.* I.5], why should so much Authority be given to it by Christ himself, who thought the Words of the Institution as there recorded ought to be the Rule & Standard according to which those Controversies were to be judged?

When he disputed with the Sadducees about the Resurrection, his main argument is drawn from the Words of Moses. *Have ye not read that which was spoken unto them by God saying, I am the God of Abraham,* etc. [Matthew 22:31], which were the Words God spoke to Moses & are recorded in the Book of Exodus [Exodus 3:15]. Where our Saviour urges the force & importance of the very Words, which he would never have done if his writings had not been genuine & sincere. And when he treats with his own Disciples he gives them not the least Discovery of any imperfection of the Books of Scripture then received. /36ʳ/ For, *beginning at Moses & all the Prophets he expounded to them in all the Scriptures the things concerning himself.* And, *all things must be fulfilled which were written in the Law of Moses & the Prophets & the Psalms concerning me* [Luke 24:27, 44]. So that upon all occasions our Saviour makes use of the Authority of the Books of Moses, as well as the other Parts of Scripture, not as confused heaps of Collections, but as Authentick declarations of the Will of God to mankind. After Christ's ascension S. Peter urges the Jews with the very words of Moses, *For Moses truely said unto the Fathers,* etc. [Acts 3:222]. And he is said by S. Stephen *to receive from God the lively Oracles to give unto us* [7:38]. Of whom the Apostles in Council *at Jerusalem say, Moses of old time hath in every Copy them that preach him being read in the Synagogue every Sabbath Day* [15:21]. And as often as they have occasion to mention, as they have frequently, the History of the Creation, & Fall of Man, of the Patriarchs, of the Deluge, of the Israelites coming out of Egypt, the giving of the Law & the Acts of Moses, they do it so exactly according to those Copies received by the Jewish & Christian Church, without any attending to amend & correct the errors & mistakes of them; that till the Authority of Christ & his Apostles be overthrown, which we are certain can never be done, the Authority of the Books of Moses must still be maintained by all the Disciples of Christ & his Apostles. For certainly none had greater reason to have discovered the imperfection of the Books of the Law, than the Apostles had, when Moses was by the Jews so vehemently set up in opposition to Christ. And therefore that dear /37ʳ/ Reverence they always shewd for him & his sacred Writings, ought to stop the Words of Cavillers, & silence the trifling Objections against the Sacred Authority of them. And so much for the clearing the writings of Moses, the first Person here mentioned in the Text, *If they hear not Moses,* etc. 2. I now come to *the Prophets*; whose Authority hath in this bold Age been attacked after another manner. It is said with Confidence enough, if that would do the Busyness, that *the Prophets were indeed a sort of innocent & vertuous men who had no ill designs, but perswaded Men to Repentance & a good Life; but they were weak, melancholy, & fanatical men who took the strong impression of their own Imaginations for the Motions & Inspirations of the Holy Ghost* [Tractatus Theol-Pol., 1–3]. But that the Opinion itself is one of the greatest & most unreasonable transports of Imagination will appear by these considerations. 1. That no force of Imagination could extend itself to such particular Events as the Prophets foretold. If the Prophets had onely attracted the people with Mystical & Enthusiastical Discourses, or general threatnings of Gods heavy judgments, there might have been some colour for this pretence; but they spake very plainly in the judgments they denounced & descended to such particulars, as to time & place & Persons as could never come from the mere force of Imagination. If there were nothing more in Prophecy but this, the World would never be without great store of Prophets, for it never wants such whose Imaginations are too strong for their /38r/ understandings. There have not wanted pretenders to the Spirit of Prophecie but either the event hath confuted their predictions; or their Works were ambiguous & capable of different senses; or some other circumstances have concurred which rendred their whole pretence suspicious. As in the case of Savonarola, the greatest Man without dispute who in these latter Ages pretended to a Spirit of Prophecy being a Person of great esteem both for his Life & Doctrine; yet some of his Predictions were apparently false as about the Conversion of the Turks & Moors in his time, the Return of Charles 8. into Italy; others had a doubtful meaning; but that which rendred the whole suspicious was that he was a busy Politick, intriguing Person, who had made himself the Head of a Potent Faction in Florence, which he governed as long as his Esteem continued. But no suspicions of this Nature can be fastend on the Prophets of old, who took no part with a Popular Faction to the disturbance of the Government; but lived quietly & peaceably & onely forewarned the People of Calamities which would certainly come upon them, if they did not in time repent of their Sins. And that not in general Terms, but told them long before it happend, the way & manner & Persons from whom they should suffer, viz. the Chaldeans by whom they should be carried into Captivity. The first time this was foretold, was when both the Kingdoms of Israel & Judah were in great Prosperity, in the time of Jeroboam King of Israel & /39ʳ/ Uzziah King of Judah; then Hosea prophesying of the ceasing of the Kingdom of Israel in no long time to come & then against all the face of Religion & Government . . . from them [Hosea 1:4, 2:11–12, 3:4]: which came exactly to passe about 70 years after. About the same time, the Prophet Amos foretells the same thing; & more expressly adds, *that they should go into Captivity beyond Damascus* [Amos 5:27, 7:11]. And in the days of Uzziah, Isaiah prophecied in Judah, & he foretells a Captivity there too; & exactly describes the Chaldeans, by their Distance, their Motion, their Arrows, & the Power of the Nation: & afterwards calls *the Assyrian the Rod of Gods Anger;* & saith *that God would send him against a hypocritical Nation* [Isaiah 5:26–29; 10: 5–6]. When Sennacherib came up against Jerusalem, then the King & people thought the great desolation so long threatend was coming upon them. The Prophet tells them No; *for he should soon return & be killed in his own Land* [37:6–7]; which was exactly fulfilled. But afterwards he tells Hezekiah *that his Treasures should be carried to Babylon, & his Sons should serve as Eunuchs there* [39:6–7]; which must needs be an astonishing Prophecy to him, but was accordingly accomplished. The same thing continued to be told by the following Prophets to the very time of the Captivity. Neither did they onely prophecy concerning Judah; but so particularly concerning the Fates of Moab & Tyre & Egypt & Babylon, & other . . . Nations so agreeably to the Histories of those Times [16:14, 23:15, 17, 19:2, 13:19], that there seems to be no tolerable evasion but that of Prophecie concerning Daniels /38ᵛ/ remarkable Prophecy of the Four Monarchies /39ʳ/ that the Prophecies were made after the things were done; which is to overthrow /40ʳ/ the Faith of all History, & to believe not according to Reason but merely by Humour & inclination. But what can be said for the Prophets foretelling the exact time of the Jews return from their Captivity at the end of LXX years [Jeremiah 25:11–12]? What force of Imagination could make them pitch upon that time rather than LX or LXXX or C years? & yet the accomplishment was just at that time in the first year of Cyrus his Reign [2 Chronicles 35:22, Ezekiel 1:1]. How came the very name of Cyrus into the Imagination of Isaiah about CL years at least before he was born [Isaiah 44:28, 45:4]?

What could be more casual & arbitrary than a name? What more remote from human foresight than the Name of a Person so long before his Nativity? But before all these, what can be said to that admirable & Divine Prophecy of Isaiah concerning the humiliation & exaltation of the Messias so long before his coming into the World [Isaiah 53]? Which cannot with any shew of probability be understood either of the People of the Jews, or of Josias, or Jeremiah, or any other Persons; but that doth . . . agree with the entertainment Christ met with in the World, the wonderful Patience with which he did bear his Sufferings, with the glorious recompence he had after them. What can be said to the clear Prophecies of his coming, during the 2nd Temple, when it was but newly built & hath now been so long destroyd [Haggai 2:7–9, Malachiah 3:1]? What to the limitation of the time by Daniel for the coming of the Messias [Daniel 9:24], & the destruction of the City & Sanctuary, which was to be accomplished within the LXX Weeks, or 490 years? From what /41^r/ edict soever they commence, whether of Cyrus, or Darius, or Artaxerxes; wheresoever they had their exact accomplishment; as long as the just measure of time was fulfilled, this Prophecy alone will confute all the vain offences of Scepticks & unbelievers. for it is impossible that ever a man by the force of Imagination should be able to fix the bounds of time with that exactness, wherewith they are set down in that Prophecy. But by this we see what miserable shifts the most philosophical & subtle defenders of the cause of Infidelity in this Age are driven to; & it cannot but be a great satisfaction to the minds of good Men, to see how little Reason they have on their side, when they dare to speak their Minds. 2. If we examin all the Discourses of the Prophets there is so much not onely of vertue & Goodness but of Reason & consistency both with themselves & with each other, that no one who hath Understanding himself can attribute them to the heats & transports of Imagination. They never fell into raving & involuntary Madness, as the Pythian Prophetesses & Sibylls did; nor into such extatick Raptures, as Montanus & Maximilla & other Enthusiasts have done. The Spirit of Prophecy never blinded their Understandings, nor took from them the Use of their Reason; the things they spake were divine, but they delivered them after the manner of Men, with judgment & temper. They spake with great Authority & Gentleness, with a commanding force of Reason, but with that affection & tenderness as shewd

they regarded more the Good of the /42ʳ/ People then their own Authority. At times they were unreasonably displeasd with them, & set up
the false Prophets against them; because they flatterd and humourd them
in their pleasing Sins, & promised them Peace & Prosperity notwithstanding them; by which means their Work was rendred more difficult &
unpleasing to themselves; but they were not discouraged by all the ill
Usage & Reproaches they met with; which they did bear with invincible
Patience & a serene Courage & went on & did their duty with great
fidelity & sincerity. And although they . . . the good opinion of those
they lived amongst was seldom gained, & soon lost, & hardly recoverd;
yet like wise Physicians they regarded more the Good of their Patients
than their good Opinion. & went on still to perswade men to Repent of
their Sins, even when they mocked them for so doing. But least it should
be thought meer sowreness & moroseness of Temper, which made them
speak so much of the dreadful Judgments of God upon them for their
Sins, they mixed & temperd their threatnings with the most gracious &
encouraging Promises of the Favours & Mercy of God to them, if they
would yet Repent. Which shews how vain & foolish that Imagination is
that the Prophets spake onely according to their natural Tempers, a chearful Tem-
per disposing them to foretell Victory & Peace, & a melancholy one wars & heavy
. . . [Tractatus Theol-Pol., p. 18], since the same Prophets in the same
discourses do very often mix them together & use them as several arguments to perswade them to the same things, which were to /43ʳ/ Repent
& amend their lives, to do justly & to love Mercy & to walk humbly with
God. They knew nothing better for Mankind to do; & therefore used the
most effectual Means to perswade them to the Practice of them. Their
busyness was not to read Lectures of Philosophy, or to resolve difficult
Problems about Lines & Numbers; it was not to busy their Heads with
Polititicks & new Frames of Government; much less to encourage Faction
& Sedition amongst the People; but their work was to convince them of
their Sins against God, & to teach & reproove & reform a very perverse &
obstinate Nation; who were scarce sensible of anything but Prosperity &
outward Troubles, & scarce of them neither at any great distance. To such
a People they used the most proper & effectual Arguments, the Wit of
Man could devise, & managed them with great force & a surprising Maj-

esty in their Expressions. If to all these things we joyn their Unanimity & Agreement among themselves in distant places & Times; we have the greatest Reason to conclude that these were not brainsick & Enthusiastical Men, full of vaporous & vain imaginations; but they were *holy Men of God who spake as they were moved by the Holy Ghost.*

Appendix II

A Chronological List of Primary Works of Anglican Scriptural Interpretation in the Seventeenth Century

THERE follows a chronological listing of some major seventeenth-century books, pamphlets, and sermons whose contents adequately represent Anglican scriptural interpretation in the century. The list is selective. The principle of inclusion has not been whether a work merely interprets or uses scriptural texts; a listing of works composed on such grounds would be far too lengthy for practical use. Rather, I have included works which in an exemplary manner offer either general principles of Anglican scriptural interpretation or methods of argument from which such principles might easily be inferred.

It is impossible to date many Anglican sermons of the later part of the century, including some that have been essential to my development of ideas in this book. For example, I have not been able to date the important series of sermons on faith by Isaac Barrow and John Tillotson, which I have extensively drawn upon in Chapter 2. If an individual sermon was not printed soon after its delivery, if later editors failed to provide dating for it in the first collected editions, and if external helps, such as the diaries of John Evelyn and Samuel Pepys, do not record the sermon, it is likely that its date is forever lost. In the matter of dating, political sermons, because they are, in the technical sense, occasional, provide the least problems.

The dates given in the left column are for the first edition only; dates in brackets signify the year a work was written if its publication was delayed. Titles of sermons are in quotation marks; titles of books and pamphlets are in italics.

1617	John Hales	"A Sermon Concerning the Abuses of Obscure and Difficult Places of Holy Scripture" (on 2 Pet. 3:16)
1638	William Chillingworth	*The Religion of Protestants a Safe Way to Salvation*
1645	Lucius Cary, Viscount Falkland	*Of the Infallibility of the Church of Rome*
[1647]	Edward Hyde	*Contemplations and Reflections upon the Psalms of David* (on Pss. 1–70)
1657	Brian Walton, ed.	*Biblia Sacra Polyglotta*
[1658]	John Lightfoot	"A Sermon Preached at St. Michael Cornhill" (on John 10:22–23)
1659	Brian Walton	*The Considerator Considerated, or A Brief View of Certain Considerations upon the Biblia Sacra Polyglotta*
1660	John Pearson	*No Necessity of Reformation of the Public Doctrine of the Church of England*
[1660]	Robert South	"The Scribe Instructed" (on Matt. 12:52)
1661	Robert Boyle	*Some Considerations Touching the Style of the Holy Scriptures*
1662	Edward Stillingfleet	*Origines Sacrae, or A Rational Account of the Christian Faith*
[1663]	Robert South	"A Sermon Preached at Westminster Abbey" (on Rom. 13:5)
1666	John Tillotson	*The Rule of Faith*
1667	Thomas Sprat	*The History of the Royal Society of London for the Improving of Natural Knowledge*
1669	Edward Stillingfleet	*A Discourse Concerning the Sufferings of Christ*
[1669]	Edward Stillingfleet	"The Sin and Danger of Rebellion" (on Jude 1:11)
1670	Thomas Tenison	*The Creed of Mr. Hobbes Examined*
[1671]	Edward Hyde	*Contemplations and Reflections upon the Psalms of David* (on Pss. 71–150)
1672	Charles Wolseley	*The Reasonableness of Scripture Belief*

1672	Seth Ward	"An Apology for the Mysteries of the Gospel" (on Rom. 1:16)
[1673]	Richard Allestree	"The Divine Authority and Usefulness of the Holy Scripture" (on 2 Tim. 3:15)
[1673]	Isaac Barrow	"A Sermon on the Gunpowder Plot" (on Ps. 54:9–10)
1675	Gilbert Burnet	*A Rational Method for Proving the Truth of the Christian Religion*
[1675]	Robert South	"The Peculiar Care and Concern of Providence for the Protection and Defence of Kings" (on Ps. 144:10)
1675	John Wilkins	*Of the Principles and Duties of Natural Religion*
1676	Joseph Glanvill	*Essays on Several Important Subjects in Philosophy and Religion*
1678	William Sancroft	"A Sermon Preached to the House of Peers on 13 November 1678" (on Ps. 57:1)
1678	Edward Stillingfleet	"A Sermon Preached on the Fast Day, 13 November 1678 . . . to the House of Commons" (on 1 Sam. 12:24–25)
[1679–80]	John Locke	*Two Treatises of Government* (published 1690)
1681	John Dryden	*Absalom and Achitophel*
1681	Samuel Parker	*A Demonstration of the Divine Authority of the Law of Nature and of the Christian Religion*
1682	John Dryden	*Religio Laici, or A Layman's Faith*
1683	Simon Patrick	*A Discourse about Tradition*
[1683]	Edward Stillingfleet	"Sermon on Luke 19:31" (See Appendix I)
1683	Thomas Tenison	*A Discourse Concerning a Guide in Matters of Faith*
1684	John Lightfoot	*Horae Hebraicae et Talmudicae in Quattuor Evangelistas*

1685	Robert Filmer	*Patriarcha, or the Natural Power of Kings,* 2d ed.
1685	Edward Pococke	*A Commentary on the Prophecy of Hosea*
1687	Edward Stillingfleet	"Scripture and Tradition Compared" (on Col. 2:6)
1691	Edward Pococke	*A Commentary of the Prophecy of Joel*
1691	Edward Stillingfleet	"The Mysteries of the Christian Faith Asserted and Vindicated" (on 1 Tim. 1:15)
1692	William Lowth	*A Vindication of the Divine Authority and Inspiration of the Writings of the Old and New Testament*
1692	Edward Pococke	*A Commentary on the Prophecy of Malachi* and *A Commentary on the Prophecy of Micah*
1693–95	John Edwards	*A Discourse Concerning the Authority, Style and Perfection of the Books of the Old and New Testament*
1693	Edward Stillingfleet	"A Sermon Preached before the King and Queen at Whitehall, Christmas Day, 1693" (on John 3:17)
[1693]	John Tillotson	"The Duty and Reason of Praying for Governors" (on 1 Tim. 2:12)
1693	John Tillotson	*Sermons Concerning the Divinity and Incarnation of Our Blessed Saviour* (delivered 1679–80)
1693	John Tillotson	"A Sermon Concerning the Unity of the Divine Nature and the Blessed Trinity" (on 1 Tim. 2:5) and "A Sermon Preached before the Queen at Whitehall, Concerning the Sacrifice and Satisfaction of Christ" (on Heb. 9:26)
1694	Gilbert Burnet	*Four Discourses Delivered to the Clergy of the Diocese of Sarum*
1694	Gilbert Burnet	"A Sermon Preached at the Funeral of

the Most Reverend Father in God, the
Late John, by the Divine Providence,
Archbishop of Canterbury" (on 2
Tim. 4:7)

1694   Richard Kidder

*A Commentary on the Five Books of
Moses*

[1694]   Robert South

"Christianity Mysterious and the Wisdom of God in Making It So" (on 1
Cor. 2:7)

1695   John Locke

*The Reasonableness of Christianity as
Delivered in the Scriptures*

1696   Edward Stillingfleet

*A Discourse Concerning the Doctrine of
Christ's Satisfaction*

1697   George Stanhope

"The Perfection of Scripture Stated
and Its Sufficiency Argued" (on 1
Tim. 3:16–17)

1697   Edward Stillingfleet

A Discourse in Vindication of the Doctrine of the Trinity

1698   Simon Patrick

*A Commentary on the First Book of
Moses*

1699   Gilbert Burnet

An Exposition of the Thirty-Nine Articles of the Church of England

1700   John Richardson

*The Canon of the New Testament
Vindicated*

[1700?]   John Locke

*A Paraphrase and Notes on the Epistles of
Paul . . . To Which Is Prefixed An Essay
for the Understanding of St. Paul's
Epistles, by Considering St. Paul Himself*

Abbreviations

Barrow	Isaac Barrow, *Works*, 4 vols. (London, 1683–87).
Leviathan	Thomas Hobbes, *Leviathan*, ed. Michael Oakeshott (Oxford: Basil Blackwell, 1946).
Locke	John Locke, *Works*, 10 vols. (London, 1823).
OS	Edward Stillingfleet, *Origines Sacrae*, 3d ed. (London, 1666).
RF	John Tillotson, *The Rule of Faith* (London, 1666).
RP	William Chillingworth, *The Religion of Protestants* (Oxford, 1638).
South	Robert South, *Sermons*, 11 vols. (London, 1692–1744).
Stillingfleet	Edward Stillingfleet, *Works*, 6 vols. (London, 1707, 1709, 1710, 1709, 1709, 1710).
Tillotson	John Tillotson, *Sermons*, 14 vols. (London, 1695–1704).
Tractatus	Spinoza, *Tractatus Theologico-Politicus*, trans. R.H.M. Elwes (1883; rpt. New York: Dover Publications, 1951).

Notes

Preface

1. Samuel Pepys, *The Diary*, ed. Robert Latham and William Matthews, 10 vols. (Berkeley and Los Angeles: University of California Press, 1970–83), 1:158.
2. *RP*, p. 115.
3. The three best studies of Anglican theology in the period are Phillip Harth, *Swift and Anglican Rationalism* (Chicago: University of Chicago Press, 1961); H. R. McAdoo, *The Spirit of Anglicanism: A Survey of Anglican Theological Method in the Seventeenth Century* (London: Adam and Charles Black, 1965); and Irène Simon, *Three Restoration Divines: Barrow, South, and Tillotson*, 2 vols. in 3, Bibliothêque de la Faculté de Philosophie et Lettres de l'Université de Liège, facs. CLXXI, CCXIII (Paris: Societé d'Edition "Les Belles Lettres," 1967, 1976). See also Robert S. Bosher, *The Making of the Restoration Settlement: The Influence of the Laudians, 1649–1662* (New York: Oxford University Press, 1951); Gerald R. Cragg, *From Puritanism to the Age of Reason* (Cambridge: The University Press, 1950); Horton Davies, *Worship and Theology in England*, vol. 2, *From Andrewes to Baxter and Fox, 1603–1690* (Princeton: Princeton University Press, 1975); I. M. Green, *The Re-establishment of the Church of England, 1660–63* (Oxford: Oxford University Press, 1978); R. Buick Knox, "The History of Doctrine in the Seventeenth Century," in *A History of Christian Doctrine*, ed. Hubert Cunliffe-Jones (Philadelphia: Fortress Press, 1978); Henry G. Van Leeuwen, *The Problem of Certainty in English Thought, 1630–1690* (The Hague: Martinus Nijhoff, 1963); J. Wickham Legg, *English Church Life from the Restoration to the Tractarian Movement* (New York: Longmans Green, 1914); John Redwood, *Reason, Ridicule, and Religion: The Age of Enlightenment in England, 1660–1750* (Cambridge, Mass.: Harvard University Press, 1976); James D. Roberts, *From Puritanism to Platonism in Seventeenth-Century England* (The Hague: Martinus Nijhoff, 1968); Barbara J. Shapiro, *Probability and Certainty in Seventeenth-Century England* (Princeton: Princeton University Press, 1983); Norman Sykes, *From Sheldon to Secker: Aspects of*

English Church History, 1660–1768 (Cambridge: Cambridge University Press, 1959); John Tulloch, *Rational Theology and Christian Philosophy in England in the Seventeenth Century*, 2 vols. (Edinburgh: William Blackwood, 1872); and Jan Walgrave, *Unfolding Revelation* (Philadelphia: Westminster Press, 1972).

Because much theology of late seventeenth-century England is enunciated in sermons, the following studies of preaching may interest the reader: *The Classic Preachers of the English Church*, ed. J. E. Kempe, 2 vols. (London, 1877–78); Rolf P. Lessenich, *Elements of Pulpit Oratory in Eighteenth-Century England (1660–1800)* (Cologne: Bohlan Verlag, 1972); W. Fraser Mitchell, *English Pulpit Oratory from Andrewes to Tillotson* (1932; rpt. New York: Russell and Russell, 1962); and Caroline F. Richardson, *English Preachers and Preaching, 1640–1670* (New York: Macmillan, 1928).

4. Leslie Stephen, *History of English Thought in the Eighteenth Century*, 2 vols., 3d ed. (London: Smith and Elder, 1902), 1:76.

5. Mark Pattison, "Tendencies of Religious Thought in England, 1688–1750," in *Essays*, 2 vols. (Oxford: Clarendon Press, 1889), 2:48.

6. See, for example, Robert E. Sullivan, *John Toland and the Deist Controversy: A Study in Adaptations* (Cambridge, Mass.: Harvard University Press, 1982), chap. 2.

7. For a further discussion see my "Socinians, John Toland, and the Anglican Rationalists," *Harvard Theological Review* 70 (1977): 287–89.

Chapter 1: A Moment in Scriptural Interpretation

1. Basil Hall, "Biblical Scholarship: Editions and Commentaries," in *The Cambridge History of the Bible*, vol. 3, *The West from the Reformation to the Present Day*, ed. S. L. Greenslade (Cambridge: Cambridge University Press, 1963), p. 64.

2. See *Memoirs of the Life and Writing of the Right Rev. Brian Walton*, ed. Henry John Todd, 2 vols. (London, 1821), 1:47.

3. Ibid., p. 85.

4. On his title page, Toland quotes Tillotson's dictum: "Nor need we to desire a better Evidence, that any Man is in the wrong, than to hear him declare against Reason, and thereby acknowledge that Reason is against him" (*Christianity Not Mysterious* [London, 1696], sig. A1ʳ). Toland did not have to read extensively to find this quotation, which appears in volume 1 of Tillotson's *Sermons* (1695), p. 69. In context, Tillotson argues that Christianity is reasonable because God has revealed it and we can prove that he did so (ibid., pp. 68–69). *Christianity Not Mysterious* argues against the use of such a methodology and in favor of internal rational proofs of Scripture. Toland thus uses

a quote from Tillotson which, in its contextual meaning, opposes the thrust of Toland's 1696 work.

5. For a discussion of Chillingworth's definition of reason, see Robert R. Orr, *Reason and Authority: The Thought of William Chillingworth* (Oxford: Clarendon Press, 1967), chap. 4.

6. *Tractatus*, p. 195.

7. For Tillotson's career at St. Lawrence Jewry, see Gilbert Burnet, *A Sermon Preached at the Funeral of the Most Reverend Father in God, John, by the Divine Providence, Lord Archbishop of Canterbury* (London, 1694), pp. 19–20, and Thomas Birch, *The Life of the Most Reverend Dr. John Tillotson* (London, 1752), pp. 27–28. For Stillingfleet's sermon, see "The Mysteries of the Christian Faith Asserted and Vindicated," in Stillingfleet, 1:452–66.

8. See Stillingfleet, 3:446–47, 470–71.

9. See Birch, *Life*, pp. 211, 352, 445–46; and G. M. Webster, "The Life and Opinions of Robert South, D.D." (B.D. thesis, Exeter College, Oxford, 1951), pp. vii, 168.

10. Stillingfleet, 5:71 (sig. 14^r, following pp. 1–128).

11. Samuel Butler, *Hudibras*, ed. John Wilders (Oxford: Clarendon Press, 1967), pp. 6–7.

12. See Irène Simon, *Three Restoration Divines: Barrow, South, and Tillotson*, 2 vols. in 3, Bibliothèque de la Faculté de Philosophie et Lettres de l'Université de Liège, facs. CLXXI, CCXIII (Paris: Societé d'Edition "Les Belles Lettres," 1967, 1976), 1:1–73; and Horton Davies, *Worship and Theology in England*, vol. 2, *From Andrewes to Baxter and Fox, 1603–1690* (Princeton: Princeton University Press, 1975), chap. 4.

13. For recent surveys, see Michael McKeon, *Politics and Poetry in Restoration England: The Case of Dryden's Annus Mirabilis* (Cambridge, Mass.: Harvard University Press, 1975), pt. 2, passim; and Margaret C. Jacob, *The Newtonians and the English Revolution, 1689–1720* (Ithaca: Cornell University Press, 1976), chap. 3.

14. Mark Pattison, "Tendencies of Religious Thought in England, 1688–1750," *Essays*, 2 vols. (Oxford: Clarendon Press, 1889), 2:48.

15. Tillotson, 12:75.

16. Descartes, *A Discourse on Method, Meditations on the First Philosophy, and The Principles of Philosophy* (London: Dent, 1978), p. 175.

17. Especially because of their relation to the development of the New Science after 1660, the divines' theories of certainty and probability have formed the most researched aspect of their thought. For the most recent treatments, see Barbara J. Shapiro, *Probability and Certainty in Seventeenth-Century England* (Princeton: Princeton University Press, 1983), chap. 3, and Michael Hunter, *Science and Society in Restoration England* (Cambridge: Cambridge University Press, 1981), chap. 7.

18. Jan Walgrave, *Unfolding Revelation* (Philadelphia: Fortress Press, 1972), p. 195.

Chapter 2: The Argument from Internal Evidence

1. Edward Lord Herbert of Cherbury, *De Religione Laici*, ed. and trans. Harold R. Hutcheson (New Haven: Yale University Press, 1944), p. 99.
2. Ibid., p. 129.
3. Edward Lord Herbert of Cherbury, *De Veritate*, trans. and intro. Meyrick H. Carré (Bristol: J. W. Arrowsmith, 1937), p. 290.
4. *The Life of Edward, First Lord Herbert of Cherbury*, ed. J. M. Shuttleworth (London: Oxford University Press, 1976), p. 31.
5. Edward Lord Herbert of Cherbury, *De Veritate*, pp. 291, 303–5.
6. For further comment on Herbert and revelation, see R. D. Bedford, *The Defence of Truth: Herbert of Cherbury and the Seventeenth Century* (Manchester: Manchester University Press, 1979), pp. 136–57.
7. Paul J. Johnson, "Hobbes's Anglican Doctrine of Salvation," in *Thomas Hobbes in His Time*, ed. Ralph Ross, Herbert W. Schneider, and Theodore Waldman (Minneapolis: University of Minnesota Press, 1974), pp. 114–15; for a view of the sincerity of Hobbes's theism, see Willis B. Glover, "God and Thomas Hobbes," in *Hobbes Studies*, ed. K. C. Brown (Oxford: Basil Blackwell, 1965), pp. 141–68.
8. John Hales, *Works*, 3 vols. (Glasgow, 1765), 2:17.
9. *Leviathan*, p. 50.
10. Ibid., p. 387.
11. Ibid., pp. 41–42, 254.
12. Spinoza's *Tractatus Theologico-Politicus* was published anonymously in Hamburg in 1670; another edition, with no place of publication on the title page and with supplementary material by the author, was published in 1674. The first English translation—by an anonymous translator—was *A Treatise Partly Theological, and Partly Political* (London, 1689), although *Miracles No Violations of the Laws of Nature* (London, 1683), a free translation of, among other things, chapter 6 of the *Tractatus*, appeared six years earlier. For background on Spinozism in England, see Rosalie L. Colie, "Spinoza and the Early English Deists," *Journal of the History of Ideas* 20 (1959): 23–46, and "Spinoza in England, 1665– 1730," *Proceedings of the American Philosophical Society* 107 (1963): 183–219.
13. *Tractatus*, p. 187.
14. Ibid., p. 117.
15. Ibid., pp. 121, 33, 138.
16. Ibid., pp. 104, 176, 183, 185, 190–95, 189, 198.
17. John Toland, *Christianity Not Mysterious* (London, 1696), pp. 46, xxvii, 49, 27.
18. Joseph Glanvill, *Essays on Several Important Subjects in Philosophy and Religion* (London, 1676), 4:8–9, 35–36.

19. Ibid., 5:7–9.
20. *Leviathan*, p. 41.
21. Barrow, 2:55–56.
22. Stillingfleet, 4:196–97.
23. Tillotson, 12:16, 20.
24. For the more traditional view, see South, 3:227.
25. Tillotson, 12:21–28. For further discussion of the problem of certainty, see Barbara J. Shapiro, *Probability and Certainty in Seventeenth-Century England* (Princeton: Princeton University Press, 1983), pp. 94–101.
26. Barrow, 2:20.
27. Stillingfleet, 2:68–69 (sig. K1^v–2^r, following pp. 1–386).
28. Tillotson, 12:33–35.
29. Stillingfleet, 2:83–99 (sigs. M1^r–O1^r, following pp. 1–386).
30. Barrow, 2:520.
31. *OS*, p. 362.
32. For further discussion, see Frederick Coplestone, S.J., *A History of Philosophy*, vol. 5: *Hobbes to Hume* (London: Burns, Oates, and Washbourne, 1959), pp. 52–66; *The Cambridge Platonists*, ed. Gerald R. Cragg (New York: Oxford University Press, 1968), pp. 3–31; and *The Cambridge Platonists*, ed. C. A. Patrides (Cambridge, Mass.: Harvard University Press, 1970), pp. 1–41. For comparison between the Latitudinarians and Cambridge Platonists, see Norman Sykes, *From Sheldon to Secker: Aspects of English Church History, 1660–1768* (Cambridge: Cambridge University Press, 1959), pp. 140–52.
33. Tillotson, 6:102, 104.
34. Ibid., pp. 106–7.
35. Stillingfleet, 3:282.
36. Ibid., p. 292.
37. *OS*, sig. b3^r, my emphasis.
38. Ibid., p. 15.
39. Ibid., pp. 26–30, 41, 60–62, 19.
40. Ibid., p. 72.
41. Thomas Burnet, *The Sacred Theory of the Earth*, 2d ed. (London, 1691), p. 17. For the context of Burnet's work and for new bibliographical evidence, see Margaret C. Jacob, *The Newtonians and the English Revolution, 1689–1720* (Ithaca: Cornell University Press, 1976), pp. 107–19.
42. Burnet, *Theory of the Earth*, pp. 52–53, 68–70. For further discussion of Burnet's theory, see Marjorie Hope Nicolson, *Mountain Gloom and Mountain Glory* (Ithaca: Cornell University Press, 1959), pp. 195–206.
43. Thomas Burnet, *A Review of the Theory of the Earth* (London, 1690), p. 44.
44. Thomas Burnet, *Archaeologiae Philosophicae, or the Ancient Doctrine Concerning the Originals of Things* (London, 1692), pp. 42, 50.

45. Herbert Croft, *Some Animadversions upon a Book Entituled The Theory of the Earth* (London, 1685), pp. 75, 175.
46. John Beaumont, *Considerations on a Book Entitled The Theory of the Earth* (London, 1693), pp. 184–86.
47. Burnet, *Review*, pp. 45, 37.
48. Thomas Burnet, *An Answer to the Latest Exceptions Made by Mr. Erasmus Warren to the Theory of the Earth* (London, 1690), p. 84.
49. Burnet, *Review*, p. 46.

Chapter 3: Testimony and Other Arguments

1. South, 9:246–47. For a recent and full discussion of miracles as part of theological argument at the time, see R. M. Burns, *The Great Debate on Miracles* (Lewisburg: Bucknell University Press, 1981), chaps. 1 and 3.
2. Tillotson, 5:10–11, 13.
3. South, 5:340.
4. *RP*, p. 220.
5. Ralph Cudworth, *The True Intellectual System of the Universe* (London, 1678), pp. 708–9; Henry More, *Theological Works* (London, 1707), p. 769.
6. John Wilkins, *Of the Principles and Duties of Natural Religion* (London, 1675), p. 402.
7. *Leviathan*, pp. 247–49; *Tractatus*, pp. 121–27.
8. *OS*, pp. 113–20.
9. *Tractatus*, p. 127.
10. *OS*, pp. 137–39.
11. Thomas Tenison, *The Creed of Mr. Hobbes Examined* (London, 1670), p. 168.
12. Richard Kidder, *A Commentary on the Five Books of Moses: With a Dissertation Concerning the Author or Writer of the Said Books; and a General Argument to Each of Them*, 2 vols. (London, 1694), 1:LVIII–IX, LXXIV; Jean LeClerc, *Twelve Dissertations out of Mr. LeClerk's Genesis*, trans. Mr. Brown (London, 1696), pp. 114, 133. For a discussion of LeClerc in particular and Dutch theology in this period in general, see Rosalie L. Colie, *Light and Enlightenment: A Study of the Cambridge Platonists and the Dutch Arminians* (Cambridge: Cambridge University Press, 1957), esp. pp. 31–35, 109–14.
13. Kidder, *Commentary*, 1:LXXVIII–LXXX.
14. LeClerc, *Dissertations*, pp. 123, 128.
15. Kidder, *Commentary*, 1:LXXIV, LXXX; LeClerc, *Dissertations*, p. 129.
16. LeClerc, *Dissertations*, pp. 129–30.
17. See Chapter 5, for LeClerc's attempts to minimize the role of inspiration in scriptural truth.

18. *RF*, p. 183. For a thorough study of Tillotson's ideas of certainty, see Henry G. Van Leeuwen, *The Problem of Certainty in English Thought, 1630–1690* (The Hague: Mouton, 1963), pp. 32–48.

19. Samuel Parker, *A Demonstration of the Divine Authority of the Law of Nature and of the Christian Religion* (London, 1681), p. 179.

20. Charles Wolseley, *The Reasonableness of Scripture Belief* (London, 1672), pp. 262–63.

21. *RF*, p. 285.

22. *RP*, p. 61.

23. John Owen, *Of the Divine Originall, Authority, Self-Evidencing Light and Power of the Scriptures* (Oxford, 1659), p. 103. Engaged in controversy about other matters with Owen in 1659, Brian Walton expressed shock that Owen should reject the argument from miracles; see *The Considerator Considered* (1659), in *Memoirs of the Life and Writing of the Right Rev. Brian Walton*, ed. Henry John Todd (London, 1821), 2:24–25.

24. G. M. Webster, "Life and Opinions of Robert South, D.D." (B.D. thesis, Exeter College, Oxford, 1951), pp. 5, 28.

25. See Stillingfleet, "Of the Mischief of Separation" and *The Unreasonableness of Separation* (1:274–300; 2:439–674); and John Owen, *A Brief Vindication of the Non-Conformists from the Charge of Schisme* (London, 1680), and *An Enquiry into the Original, Nature, Institution, Power, Order, and Communion of the Evangelical Churches* (London, 1681).

26. Tillotson, *A Sermon Concerning the Unity of the Divine Nature* (London, 1693), pp. 18–19.

27. Barrow, 2:191.

28. George Bright, "Preface," *The Works of John Lightfoot, D.D.*, 2 vols., 1 (London, 1684), sig. b2^r.

29. Gilbert Burnet, *An Exposition of the Thirty-Nine Articles of the Church of England* (London, 1699), pp. 91–96; Tillotson, 3:25–42. For a full discussion of Messianic prophecies, see Richard Kidder, *A Demonstration of the Messias*, 3 vols. (London, 1684–1700), pt. 1.

30. Cudworth, *True Intellectual System*, p. 715.

31. Wolseley, *Reasonableness of Scripture Belief*, p. 80.

32. *RP*, p. 58.

33. *OS*, p. 251.

34. Tillotson, 12:121, 129.

35. South, 11:238.

36. John R. Knott, *The Sword of the Spirit: Puritan Responses to the Bible* (Chicago: University of Chicago Press, 1980), p. 40.

37. *The Correspondence of John Locke*, ed. E. S. DeBeer, 8 vols. (Oxford: Clarendon Press, 1976–), 5:232, 212. I quote the editor's rendering of the Latin original.

38. Ibid., pp. 212, 214, 218.
39. *The Works of John Dryden*, vol. 2, ed. H. T. Swedenberg (Berkeley and Los Angeles: University of California Press, 1972), pp. 113–14.
40. Wolseley, *Reasonableness of Scripture Belief*, p. 263. For Wolseley's influence on Dryden, see Phillip Harth, *Contexts of Dryden's Thought* (Chicago: University of Chicago Press, 1968), chap. 4 and Appendix.
41. Isaac Barrow, *Theological Works*, ed. Alexander Napier, 9 vols. (London, 1859), 7:22. The quotation is from Barrow's "Exposition on the Creed," a work overlooked by Tillotson in preparing the 1683–87 edition (7:sig. A3ʳ).

Chapter 4: Scripture and Polity

1. Edmund Ludlow, *Memoirs*, ed. C. H. Firth, 2 vols. (Oxford: Clarendon Press, 1894), 1:246.
2. *The Bible* (Amsterdam, 1640), separate pagination for Psalms, p. 52.
3. See. J. A. Mazzeo, "Cromwell as Davidic King," *Renaissance and Seventeenth-Century Studies* (New York: Columbia University Press, 1964), pp. 183–208; and Gerard Reedy, S.J., "Mystical Politics: The Imagery of Charles II's Coronation," in *Studies in Change and Revolution*, ed. Paul J. Korshin (Menston, Yorkshire: Scolar Press, 1972), pp. 24–26.
4. See Steven N. Zwicker, "Politics and Panegyric: The Figural Mode from Marvell to Pope," in *Literary Uses of Typology from the Late Middle Ages to the Present*, ed. Earl Miner (Princeton: Princeton University Press, 1977), pp. 128–41.
5. See George Morley, *A Sermon Preached at the Magnificent Coronation of the Most High and Mighty Charles IId* (London, 1661), p. 58; the best available text of Waller's "On St. James's Park, as Lately Improved by His Majesty" may be found in Earl Miner, *The Cavalier Mode from Jonson to Cotton* (Princeton: Princeton University Press, 1971), pp. 312–16.
6. Edward Hyde, *The History of the Rebellion and Civil Wars in England*, ed. W. Dunn Macray, 6 vols. (Oxford: Clarendon Press, 1888), 6:143.
7. See Robert Filmer, *Patriarcha and Other Political Works*, ed. Peter Laslett (Oxford: Basil Blackwell, 1949), p. 44; a revision of Laslett's dating of *Patriarcha*, together with a new attempt to set it in its historical context, has been undertaken by John M. Wallace, "The Date of Sir Robert Filmer's *Patriarcha*," *Historical Journal* 23 (1980): 155–65.
8. Filmer, *Patriarcha*, p. 11.
9. Besides this main argument, Filmer has a subsidiary argument from human nature. See *Patriarcha*, p. 18, and J. N. Figgis, *The Divine Right of Kings*, 2d ed. (Cambridge: Cambridge University Press, 1914), pp. 148–50.

10. Filmer, *Patriarcha*, p. 64.
11. Ibid., pp. 11–12.
12. See Gordon J. Schochet, *Patriarchalism in Political Thought: The Authoritarian Family and Political Speculation and Attitudes Especially in Seventeenth-Century England* (New York: Basic Books, 1975), p. 122; and James Daly, *Sir Robert Filmer and English Political Thought* (Toronto: University of Toronto Press, 1979), p. 57.
13. *The Works of John Dryden*, vol. 2, ed. H. T. Swedenberg (Berkeley and Los Angeles: University of California Press, 1972), p. 33.
14. John Locke, *Two Treatises of Government*, 2d ed., ed. Peter Laslett (Cambridge: Cambridge University Press, 1967), pp. 186–87.
15. Ibid., pp. 181, 183, 241.
16. Ibid., p. 288.
17. Ibid., pp. 303–4.
18. Ibid., p. 309.
19. Ibid., pp. 414–15; for other uses of scriptural evidence in the second treatise, see pp. 313–14, 321, 338, 358–59, 404, 418, 445.
20. Robert Filmer, *Patriarcha: Or the Natural Power of Kings*, ed. and intro. Edmund Bohun (London, 1685), sig. (d2)ᵛ.
21. Algernon Sidney, *Discourses Concerning Government, with His Letters, Trial, Apology, and Some Memoirs of His Life* (London, 1763), pp. 16–17.
22. Ibid., pp. 96–102, 230–31.
23. James Tyrell, *Patriarcha non Monarcha, the Patriarch Unmonarch'd* (London, 1681), p. 10. For comment on the relationship between Tyrell and Locke, see *The Correspondence of John Locke*, ed. E. S. DeBeer, 8 vols. (Oxford: Clarendon Press, 1976–), 1:xxii–xxiii.
24. Tyrell, *Patriarcha non Monarcha*, p. 97.
25. Thomas Rymer, *A General Draught and Prospect of Government in Europe . . .* (London, 1681), pp. 4–6.
26. Ibid., p. 5.
27. Edward Hyde, *Contemplations and Reflections upon the Psalms of David*, in *A Collection of Several Tracts of the Right Honorable Edward, Earl of Clarendon* (London, 1727), p. 380.
28. Ibid., pp. 669–70.
29. William Sancroft, *A Sermon Preach'd to the House of Peers, November 13th 1678* [on Psalm 57:1] (London, 1681), p. 2.
30. Tillotson, 14:161–62.
31. Christopher Hill, *Some Intellectual Consequences of the English Revolution* (London: Weidenfield and Nicholson, 1980), p. 44.
32. Irène Simon, *Three Restoration Divines: Barrow, South, and Tillotson*, 2 vols. in 3, Bibliothêque de la Faculté de Philosophie et Lettres de l'Université de Liège, facs. CLXXI, CCXXIII (Paris: Societé d'Edition "Les Belles Lettres," 1967, 1976), 1:194–95.

33. For the reaction of Stillingfleet and Tillotson, see Gerald M. Straka, *Anglican Reaction to the Revolution of 1688* (Madison: University of Wisconsin History Department, 1962), pp. 40–42, 75–76; Peter M. Selo, "John Tillotson, Archbishop of Canterbury, 1630–1694: A Study in Anglican Ideology" (Ph.D. dissertation, University of Delaware, 1970), chap. 4; and Joel H. Fishman, "Edward Stillingfleet, Bishop of Worcester (1635–99): Anglican Bishop and Controversialist" (Ph.D. dissertation, University of Wisconsin, 1977), chap. 6.

34. Barrow, 1:93; South, 6:162–63.

35. Barrow, 1:144.

36. South, 5:59–60.

37. See the discussion of Raymond Brown, in *Jerome Biblical Commentary* (Englewood Cliffs, N.J.: Prentice-Hall, 1968), ch. 71, nos. 80–81.

38. Stillingfleet, 1:237, 248.

39. South, 5:353.

40. Earl Miner, *The Restoration Mode from Milton to Dryden* (Princeton: Princeton University Press, 1974), p. 134.

41. Samuel Butler, *Hudibras*, ed. John Wilders (Oxford: Clarendon Press, 1967), p. 45.

42. For other instances of satirized typology in *Hudibras*, see Paul J. Korshin, *Typologies in England, 1650–1820* (Princeton: Princeton University Press, 1982), pp. 277–82.

43. See Samuel Butler, *Prose Observations*, ed. Hugh De Quehen (Oxford: Clarendon Press, 1979), pp. xxxii–xxxiii, 309, 312, 324; for Butler's similarity to Spinoza, ibid., pp. 25, 43–44, 67–68. Problems in editing Butler's prose remains, which are inseparable from problems in determining a line of his sustained thought on any topic, are discussed by Hugh De Quehen, "Editing Butler's Manuscripts," in *Editing Seventeenth-Century Prose*, ed. D.I.B. Smith (Toronto: University of Toronto Press, 1972), pp. 71–93.

44. For contrasting estimates of how typology is used in *Absalom and Achitophel*, either as a rhetorical figure or as political and theological argument, see Ian Jack, *Augustan Satire: Intention and Idiom in English Poetry, 1660–1750* (Oxford: Clarendon Press, 1952), chap. 4, and Steven Zwicker, *Dryden's Political Poetry: The Typology of King and Nation* (Providence: Brown University Press, 1972), pp. 83–101.

45. See Michael McKeon, *Politics and Poetry in Restoration England: The Case of Dryden's Annus Mirabilis* (Cambridge, Mass.: Harvard University Press, 1975), chap. 5.

46. *The Works of John Dryden*, vol. 2, ed. H. T. Swedenberg (Berkeley and Los Angeles: University of California Press, 1972), p. 54.

47. See Leon M. Guilhamet, "Dryden's Debasement of Scripture in *Absalom and Achitophel*," *Studies in English Literature* 9 (1969): 395–413; Dustin Griffin,

"Dryden's Charles: The Ending of *Absalom and Achitophel*," *Philological Quarterly* 52 (1978): 359–82; and Michael Conlon, "The Passage on Government in Dryden's *Absalom and Achitophel*," *Journal of English and Germanic Philology* 78 (1979): 17–32.

48. *The Works of John Dryden*, 2:12, 27.
49. For a different explanation of the same facts of this poem, see Zwicker, *Dryden's Political Poetry*, pp. 91–95.
50. Griffin, "Dryden's Charles," pp. 360–62.

Chapter 5: Canon and Text

1. Stillingfleet, 4:167.
2. John Pearson, *No Necessity of Reformation of the Publick Doctrine of the Church of England* (London, 1660), p. 23. This pamphlet answers William Hamilton, *Some Necessity of Reformation of the Publick Doctrine of the Church of England* (London, 1660), who argued that the Thirty-Nine Articles should enumerate the canonical books of the New Testament.
3. See Phillip Harth, *Contexts of Dryden's Thought* (Chicago: University of Chicago Press, 1968), pp. 202–5, for an analysis of what seventeenth-century Roman Catholics meant by "nonwritten" tradition.
4. James Mumford, *The Catholic Scripturist* (London, 1686), pp. 9–103; John Sergeant, *The Third Catholick Letter* (London, 1687), p. 58.
5. Mumford, *The Catholic Scripturist*, p. 11.
6. *Leviathan*, p. 247.
7. Ibid., p. 246.
8. John Toland, *The Life of John Milton; A Complete Collection of the Historical, Political, and Miscellaneous Works of John Milton*, 3 vols. (London, 1698), 1:29.
9. John Toland, *Amyntor, or a Defence of Milton's Life* (London, 1699), pp. 20–41. For further comment on this controversy, see Robert E. Sullivan, *John Toland and the Deist Controversy: A Study in Adaptations* (Cambridge, Mass.: Harvard University Press, 1982), pp. 134–37.
10. Toland, *Amyntor*, pp. 57–58.
11. Ibid., pp. 79–80. By "Clemens," Toland apparently meant Clement of Alexandria; for comment on Clement's alleged sponsorship of noncanonical books, see B. F. Westcott, *A General Survey of the History of the Canon of the New Testament*, 7th ed. (London: Macmillan, 1896), p. 352n.
12. John Richardson, *The Canon of the New Testament Vindicated* (London, 1700), p. 31.
13. Thomas Tenison, *The Creed of Mr. Hobbes Examined* (London, 1670), pp. 176–77.

14. Samuel Parker, *A Demonstration of the Divine Authority of the Law of Nature and of the Christian Religion* (London, 1681), p. 212.
15. *RP*, p. 62; Stillingfleet, 1:399.
16. Tillotson, 12:106.
17. Gilbert Burnet, *An Exposition of the Thirty-Nine Articles of the Church of England* (London, 1699), p. 81.
18. Stillingfleet, 5:74 (sig. K1ᵛ, following pp. 1–128).
19. John Edwards, *A Discourse Concerning the Authority, Stile, and Perfection of the Books of the Old and New Testament*, 3 vols. (London, 1693–95), 1:69.
20. Burnet, *Exposition of the Thirty-Nine Articles*, p. 82.
21. William Lowth, *A Vindication of the Divine Authority and Inspiration of the Writings of the Old and New Testament* (Oxford, 1692), pp. 195–209.
22. Stillingfleet, 6:456–57.
23. Burnet, *Exposition of the Thirty-Nine Articles*, p. 85.
24. Stillingfleet, 6:407.
25. George Tavard, *The Seventeenth-Century Tradition: A Study in Recusant Theology* (Leiden: E. J. Brill, 1978), p. 215.
26. *RP*, pp. 53, 63.
27. Westcott, *General Survey of the History of the Canon of the New Testament*, p. 508.
28. Henry More, *Theological Works* (London, 1707), pp. 11–12.
29. Tillotson, 12:134. For Stillingfleet's view of the reasonableness of prophetic inspiration, see Appendix I.
30. Burnet, *Exposition of the Thirty-Nine Articles*, pp. 86–88.
31. Jean LeClerc, *Five Letters Concerning the Inspiration of the Holy Scriptures* (London, 1690), pp. 121, 38.
32. Lowth, *Vindication*, sig. a3ᵛ, pp. 45–62, 264, 282–83.
33. Ibid., pp. 19, 84, 163–64, 110–11.
34. Thomas Sprat, *The History of the Royal Society* (London, 1667), p. 24.
35. Thomas Tenison, *A Discourse Concerning a Guide in Matters of Faith* (London, 1683), p. 36.
36. Ibid., pp. 37–38.
37. Burnet, *Exposition of the Thirty-Nine Articles*, p. 85.
38. *OS*, pp. 344–45. For an earlier statement of the argument, see Walton's "Prolegomena," *Biblia Sacra Polyglotta* (London, 1657), 1:39.
39. Richard Simon, *A Critical History of the Old Testament*, trans. Henry Dickinson (London, 1682), 3:15–16.
40. Ibid., sig. (a) 1ʳ–1ᵛ, 2ʳ–2ᵛ.
41. Ibid., sig. (a) 3ᵛ–4ʳ, (b) 1ʳ, 3:1.
42. Ibid., 2:35, 58.
43. For the Anglican view of recent editions of the Vulgate, see Stillingfleet, 4:206–7, 6:551–52.

44. Simon, *Critical History of the Old Testament*, 2:96–97, 95.
45. Richard Simon, *Critical Enquiries into the Various Editions of the Bible* (London, 1684), p. 246.
46. Simon, *Critical History of the Old Testament*, 3:153.
47. Simon, *Critical Enquiries*, p. 231; *The Critical History of the Versions of the New Testament* (London, 1692), pp. 359–60.
48. Simon, *Critical History of the Old Testament*, 3:121.
49. Ibid., sig. (b) 2ʳ, (b) 3ʳ.
50. Ibid., 1:147–48.
51. Harth, *Contexts of Dryden's Thought*, p. 183.
52. See Jean Steinmann, *Richard Simon et les origines de l'exégèse biblique* (Paris: Desclée de Brouwer, 1960), 2:117–23.
53. *The Works of John Lightfoot, D.D.*, 2 vols. (London, 1684), sig. d3ʳ.
54. Edwards, *Discourse*, 1:65–66.
55. Lowth, *Vindication*, sig. b3ᵛ–4ʳ.
56. "Sermons of Bp. Stillingfleet," Ms. 0.81, St. John's College (Cambridge), fol. 32ʳ. For the sections of this sermon dealing with the scriptural criticism of Simon and Spinoza, see Appendix I.
57. Ms. 0.81, fols. 33ʳ–37ʳ.
58. Irène Simon, *Three Restoration Divines: Barrow, South, and Tillotson*, 2 vols. in 3, Bibliothèque de la Faculté de Philosophie et Lettres de l'Université de Liège, facs. CLXXI, CCXIII (Paris: Societé d'Edition "Les Belles Lettres," 1967, 1976), 1:100.
59. See *The Correspondence of John Locke*, ed. E. S. DeBeer, 8 vols. (Oxford: Clarendon Press, 1976–), 2:18, 129, 163, 742–43, 748–51; see Gabriel Bonno, *Les relations intellectuelles de Locke avec France* (Berkeley and Los Angeles: University of California Press, 1935), pp. 217–18, for a concise consideration of Simon's influence on Locke.
60. Bodleian Ms. Locke. f. 32, fols. 1–2; Locke owned two editions (1680 and 1685) of Simon's *L'histoire critique du Vieux Testament*; see John Harrison and Peter Laslett, *The Library of John Locke* (Oxford: Clarendon Press, 1971), p. 233, nos. 2673 and 2673ᵃ.
61. See Harth, *Contexts of Dryden's Thought*, chaps. 3–6, and *The Works of John Dryden*, 2:345–48.
62. *The Works of John Dryden*, 2:118.
63. Ibid.
64. Ibid., p. 119.
65. G. Douglas Atkins, *The Faith of John Dryden: Change and Continuity* (Lexington: University Press of Kentucky, 1980), p. 94.
66. *The Works of John Dryden*, 2:117.
67. Harth, *Contexts of Dryden's Thought*, p. 202.

Chapter 6: The Socinians and Locke

1. For a discussion of the problem of naming, see Herbert McLachlan, *The Story of a Nonconformist Library* (Manchester: Manchester University Press, 1923), pp. 54–56; the standard discussion of the English Socinian movement is H. John McLachlan, *Socinianism in Seventeenth-Century England* (London: Oxford University Press, 1951). A brief, helpful summary of seventeenth-century Socinianism is offered by R. Buick Knox, "The History of Doctrine in the Seventeenth Century," in *A History of Christian Doctrine*, ed. Hubert Cunliffe-Jones (Philadelphia: Fortress Press, 1978), pp. 439–40.

2. Irène Simon, *Three Restoration Divines: Barrow, South, and Tillotson*, 2 vols. in 3, Bibliothêque de la Faculté de Philosophie et Lettres de l'Université de Liège, facs. CLXXI, CCXIII (Paris: Societé d'Edition "Les Belles Lettres," 1967, 1976), 1:180; and John Redwood, *Reason, Ridicule, and Religion: The Age of Enlightenment in England, 1660–1750* (Cambridge, Mass.: Harvard University Press, 1976), p. 170.

3. Gilbert Burnet, *History of My Own Time*, ed. Osmund Airy, 2 vols. (Oxford: Clarendon Press, 1897–1900), 1:334–35.

4. Edward Hyde, *Animadversions upon a Book, Entituled Fanaticism* (London, 1673), pp. 187–88; Joseph Glanvill, *Essays on Several Important Subjects in Philosophy and Religion* (London, 1676), 5:19; Henry Hallywell, in his annotations to George Rust, *A Discourse of the Use of Reason in Matters of Religion* (London, 1683), pp. 61–62. For comment on Chillingworth's alleged Socinianism, see Robert Orr, *Reason and Authority: The Thought of William Chillingworth* (Oxford: Clarendon Press, 1967), pp. 97–99.

5. South, 1:57–58; 3:536; 4:240–42, 313–14; 5:135–36.

6. For a discussion of the authorship and contents of the tracts, see Robert Wallace, *Antitrinitarian Biography*, 3 vols. (London, 1850), 1:218–342, and McLachlan, *Story of a Nonconformist Library*, pp. 53–87; for the printing background, see H. W. Stephenson, "Thomas Firmin, 1632–1697" (D. Phil. thesis, Oxford University, 1950), pp. 509–74.

7. "An Exhortation to a Free and Impartial Enquiry into the Doctrines of Religion" (1691), p. 4, in *The Faith of One God* (1691).

8. "An Impartial Account of the Word Mystery, as It Is Taken in Holy Scripture" (1691), p. 22, in *Faith of One God*. See also comment on "mystery" in the tracts in Gerard Reedy, S.J., "Socinians, John Toland, and the Anglican Rationalists," *Harvard Theological Review* 70 (1977): 293–94.

9. See "A Short Account of the Life of John Bidle, M.A." (1691), pp. 4–5, in *Faith of One God*.

10. "Considerations on the Explications of the Doctrine of the Trinity, by Dr. Wallis . . ." (1693), p. 3, in *A Second Collection of Tracts* (1693).

11. "An Accurate Examination of the Principal Texts Usually Alledged for the Divinity of our Saviour" (1692), p. 34, in *Second Collection*.
12. "Twelve Arguments Drawn out of Scripture" (1653), p. 10, in *Faith of One God*.
13. See "The Testimonies of Irenaeus, Justin Martyr, Tertullian, Novatianus, Theophilus, Origen, Who Lived in the Two First Centuries after Christ. . ." (1691), in *Faith of One God*, and "The Judgment of the Fathers Concerning the Doctrine of the Trinity" (1695), in *A Third Collection of Tracts* (1695).
14. "The Acts of Great Athanasius" (1690), p. 4, in *Faith of One God*. See also "The Trinitarian Scheme of Religion Concerning Almighty God" (1692), p. 27, in *Second Collection*. It is unclear whether the word "infallible" in this quotation is ironic, and thus referring to Rome and its Trinitarian theology, or not so, and thus referring to a Cartesian view of human reason, which, being God-given, cannot be assailed.
15. See, for example, "Some Thoughts upon Dr. Sherlock's Vindication of the Doctrine of the Holy Trinity" (1691), in *Faith of One God*. For brief comment on the South-Sherlock controversy, see Simon, *Three Restoration Divines*, 1: 96n., 120, 248–49.
16. "The Trinitarian Scheme of Religion Concerning Almighty God," p. 27, in *Second Collection*.
17. "Considerations on the Explications of the Doctrine of the Trinity, Occasioned by Four Sermons . . ." (1694), pp. 20–21, in *Third Collection*.
18. "Some Thoughts upon Dr. Sherlock's Vindication," p. 9, in *Faith of One God*.
19. "Considerations on the Explications," p. 21, in *Third Collection*.
20. Ibid., p. 30.
21. "Considerations on the Explications," p. 6, in *Second Collection*.
22. "Twelve Arguments Drawn out of Scripture," p. 9, in *Faith of One God*.
23. "Considerations on the Explications," p. 30, in *Third Collection*.
24. "Some Thoughts upon Dr. Sherlock's Vindication," p. 18, in *Faith of One God*.
25. Stillingfleet, 1:496; see William Sherlock's rationale for writing against the Socinian tractarians in *An Apology for Writing against Socinians* (London, 1693), pp. 10–11.
26. South, 3:302–3. For an excellent summary of the divines' concept of "mystery," see South, *Animadversions upon Dr. Sherlock's Book Entituled A Vindication of the Holy and Ever-Blessed Trinity* (London, 1693), pp. 1–6.
27. South, 3:305–6.
28. Ibid., pp. 291, 301, 300.
29. John Tillotson, *Sermons Concerning the Divinity and Incarnation of Our Blessed Saviour: Preached in the Church of St. Lawrence Jewry* (London, 1693), sig. A2ʳ–2ᵛ.

30. See, for example, *The Charge of Socinianism against Dr. Tillotson Considered* (Edinburgh, 1695); *Reflections upon a Libel Lately Printed* (London, 1696), an answer to *The Charge of Socinianism*; and *A Twofold Vindication of the Late Arch-Bishop of Canterbury and of the Author of the History of Religion* (London, 1696), pp. 29–59.

31. Tillotson, *Sermons*, p. 71.

32. *DNB*, 8:46–48; McLachlan, *Story of a Nonconformist Library*, pp. 56–57, 61; and "A Reply to the Second Defence of the XXVIII Propositions," in *Third Collection*.

33. *DNB*, 19:877.

34. Tillotson, *Sermons*, pp. 149–50.

35. John Tillotson, *A Sermon Concerning the Unity of the Divine Nature and the B. Trinity* (London, 1693), p. 20, and *A Sermon Preached before the Queen at White-Hall, April the 9th, 1693. Concerning the Sacrifice and Satisfaction of Christ* (London, 1693), p. 20.

36. Tillotson, *Unity*, p. 29.

37. Tillotson, *Sermons*, pp. 38, 114, 20–21, 90, 115, 17.

38. Ibid., pp. 17–18.

39. Ibid., pp. 120–21, 91.

40. Stillingfleet, 1:453.

41. Ibid., p. 454.

42. Ibid., 3:243.

43. Ibid., pp. 281, 436–48; 1:454–56.

44. For a discussion of the controversy, see Robert Todd Carroll, *The Common-Sense Philosophy of Religion of Bishop Edward Stillingfleet, 1635–1699* (The Hague: Martinus Nijhoff, 1975), pp. 2–4, 136–42, 90–100.

45. Stillingfleet, 3:448–62, 273–74, 283–84; for a similar discussion of the lack of contradiction in the Trinity, see Tillotson, *Sermons*, pp. 117–26.

46. Stillingfleet, 3:479–82.

47. Tillotson, *Sermons*, pp. 131–42; Tillotson, *Unity*, p. 19.

48. For an excellent analysis of the charges against Locke and of the genesis of *The Reasonableness of Christianity*, see John C. Biddle, "John Locke on Christianity: His Context and His Text" (Ph.D. dissertation, Stanford University, 1972), chap. 2.

49. Herbert McLachlan, *The Religious Opinions of Milton, Locke, and Newton* (Manchester: Manchester University Press, 1941), pp. 74–114, and Maurice Cranston, *John Locke: A Biography* (New York: Macmillan, 1957), p. 390.

50. In 1829 Lord King published extracts from Locke's commonplace books which suggest he was anti-Trinitarian. For example, Locke writes, "There be a multitude of texts that deny those things of Christ which cannot be denied of God, and that affirm such things of him that cannot agree to him if he were a person of God." See Peter King, *The Life and Letters of John Locke*, new ed.

(London, 1858), p. 297; see also pp. 342–46. On the other hand, Locke publicly wrote that scriptural evidence favors a doctrine of the real satisfaction of Christ: see "A Second Vindication of *The Reasonableness of Christianity*," in Locke, 7:417–18. See also Biddle, "John Locke," pp. 56–57.

51. Locke, "Second Vindication," p. 295.
52. John Locke, *An Essay Concerning Human Understanding*, ed. Peter H. Nidditch (Oxford: Clarendon Press, 1975), pp. 687, 694.
53. John Locke, *The Reasonableness of Christianity, as Delivered in the Scriptures*, in Locke, 7:95; "Second Vindication," p. 353.
54. John Locke, "An Essay for the Understanding of St. Paul's Epistles by Consulting St. Paul Himself," in Locke, 8:13–14.
55. John Locke, "A Vindication of *The Reasonableness of Christianity*," in Locke, 7:172; "Second Vindication," pp. 276, 302, 362.
56. Locke, *Reasonableness*, p. 5.
57. Locke, "Second Vindication," p. 357; see also the moving conclusion to "An Essay for Understanding St. Paul's Epistles," Locke, 8:22–23.
58. *The Correspondence of John Locke*, ed. E. S. DeBeer, 8 vols. (Oxford: Clarendon Press, 1976–), 5:173. I quote the editor's rendering of the Latin original.
59. Locke, *Reasonableness*, p. 28.
60. Locke, "Second Vindication," pp. 356–57.
61. John Locke, "Letter Concerning Toleration," Locke, 6:56.
62. John Locke, "A Third Letter for Toleration," Locke, 6:422–23.
63. Locke, "Second Vindication," p. 305.
64. See above, Chapter 5.
65. Locke, *Reasonableness*, pp. 15–17, 28, 44, 52, 65.
66. See Richard Ashcraft, "Faith and Knowledge in Locke's Philosophy," in *John Locke: Problems and Perspectives*, ed. John W. Yolton (Cambridge: Cambridge University Press, 1969), pp. 194–223; John C. Biddle, "Locke's Critique of Innate Principles and Toland's Deism," *Journal of the History of Ideas* 37 (1976): 411–22; and J. T. Moore, "Locke's Analysis of Language and the Assent to Scripture," *Journal of the History of Ideas* 37 (1976): 707–14.
67. Ashcraft, "Faith and Knowledge in Locke's Philosophy," p. 217.
68. Locke, *Essay Concerning Human Understanding*, pp. 698, 693.
69. Stillingfleet, 3:502–20, 571–77.
70. "Mr. Locke's Reply to the Right Reverend the Lord Bishop of Worcester's Answer to His Second Letter," Locke, 4:343, 474–75.
71. Locke, *Essay Concerning Human Understanding*, pp. 690–91.
72. John Locke, "A Discourse of Miracles," Locke, 9:259. For further discussion of Locke's thought on miracles, see R. M. Burns, *The Great Debate on Miracles* (Lewisburg: Bucknell University Press, 1981), chap. 3.
73. *Correspondence of Locke*, 5:370. I quote the editor's rendering of the Latin original.

74. Locke, "Second Vindication," pp. 263, 275. See also Biddle, "John Locke," pp. 15–20.

Conclusion

1. Samuel Richardson, *Clarissa or, the History of A Young Lady*, 4 vols. (London: J. M. Dent, 1932), 2:194.
2. Arthur H. Cash, *Laurence Sterne: The Early and Middle Years* (London: Methuen, 1975), p. 212; for a detailed list of Sterne's borrowings from Tillotson, see Lansing van der Heyden Hammond, *Laurence Sterne's Sermons of Mr. Yorick* (New Haven: Yale University Press, 1948), pp. 155–76.
3. L. P. Curtis, *Anglican Moods of the Eighteenth Century* (Hamden, Conn.: Archon Books, 1966), p. 42.
4. John Henry Cardinal Newman, *Apologia Pro Vita Sua, Being a History of His Religious Opinions*, ed. Martin J. Svaglic (Oxford: Clarendon Press, 1967), pp. 55, 109, 184–86. I am indebted to Vincent Ferrer Blehl, S.J., for calling to my attention Newman's argument with the Anglican divines of the late seventeenth century.

Index